Dedicated to the 'inner you' who wants to be revealed to the world

Curiosity is an endless task, although it stirs within us an energy whose source is also endless

Contents

Preface	1
Beginning With The End In Mind	3
Phase One: Into The Mind	11
Phase Two: The Cs To Sow To See: The Four C Process: The Primary Cs	37
The Secondary Cs: The Supporting Cast & Crew	57
The Overarching C	95
Important Non-C Words For Success	105
Phase Three: Final Thoughts, Reflections & Analogies	117

<u>Preface</u>

In my experience, there is no 'one-size-fits-all' approach to life. Just as each individual on the planet past, present, and future has been, is, and will be unique, so too is everyone's path through life. Along that path, there have been and will continue to be incredibly inspiring people who can shed light on the qualities and characteristics that have helped them find their way. Their journeys are theirs and theirs alone but their thoughts, ideas, and experiences have the ability to connect with something universal within us all. If we learn something and are inspired to apply it to our own lives it becomes a part of our journey.

But for how long does this last? That depends on individuals themselves, and what they're seeking in their lives. Regardless, shared words, thoughts, ideas, experiences, etc. can offer each of us inspiration, empowerment, motivation, reflection, and so forth. The most essential aspect in life is one thing only: *action*. Without action, our thoughts, ideas, and goals are just unrealized dreams. Action is the only way to realize them and our full potential. Life is a journey of learning, personal growth, and sharing with others, all of which can occur in an infinite number of possible ways.

Even though every individual person shares the journey with others, what others receive is entirely up to them. The most influential ideas are those that transcend time. Those that connect with our spirit and make us dig deeper within ourselves to see what we're missing. The answer is always the same; that we're not actually missing anything. Whatever we thought we were was actually there all along.

This is not a book about how the world is. It is a book of how I see the world. Not of how I have seen it in the past or how I see it in the future. It is a book about the way I see things right now. Ideas, like pictures, are just snapshots of time and space except, unlike pictures, they have the ability to guide us into the future we seek.

In the same way that ideas can, the language we use and the way we communicate, have the ability to shape our reality and future. In order to move forward in our lives, if we want to achieve our full potential, we must raise our level of consciousness.

Do we see the world as it is: through a conscious state of mind? Or do we reside in the world of the unconscious mind and live out whatever it projects into our reality without us even realizing it? Do we continually see events, experiences, and people in an objective reality? Or do we always see things through our own subjective lens? And, more importantly, will we ever know the difference?

This book was born out of my realization that love, life, and possibility are present all around us. It is my life's journey and goal to help reveal this gift through empowering, enlightening, and inspiring others as they seek to recognize and embrace their own inner strengths.

Beginning With The End In Mind

Your Destination

Have you ever tried getting somewhere without a map? If we don't use one we may or may not get to our destination and if we don't it will almost definitely take longer than if we did use a map. We're so dependent on maps. We use our car GPS systems and our cellphone GPS systems, which are both extremely handy! How would we know where we're going without a map or access to a map? Our maps ensure we use the most efficient and effective route to get to our desired destination.

I'll call this *The Restaurant Analogy*. Imagine you've travelled to a different city and decide to try a new local restaurant. You have many options for how you could get there. You would walk, drive, call a cab, or go with someone else. Let's say it's a beautiful sunny afternoon and you're going to walk to the restaurant. Now, deciding to walk could be a simple task, or more difficult depending how large the city is and how close our hotel is to the restaurant.

So you get outside and start walking. You're so excited to be going to one of the highest-rated restaurants in the city. The reviews you've read online about the restaurant are fantastic! You can almost taste how delicious everything is going to be and you're already *really* hungry. Thirty minutes pass and you're still really excited although a little hungrier. One hour passes and you have yet to reach the restaurant. Now your patience is being tested but it's still beautiful and you're still excited to get there. However, the hours continue to pass, the sun is long gone, and you're still not there. Now you're tired, unmotivated, and just want something eat and to get to bed at this point. What happened?

I guess I forgot to mention that you *knew* the restaurant was in the city but you didn't actually *know where* it was and you didn't bring your phone. So you actually had *no idea* where you were walking! Absolutely None! Now, many, if not most people would say, *that's a stupid plan! What the heck were you thinking?! How did you expect to get to the restaurant if you didn't actually know where to go?!*

The fascinating tidbit here is that this is the very way many people live their lives! Then they get lost, tired, unmotivated, lonely, angry, frustrated and then they themselves wonder, *how did I get here?* But it doesn't stop there. They don't take a look at their own tactics as to how they've arrived at the destination they 'apparently' didn't want. They'll look for circumstances or people or experiences or events to lay the blame on, instead of taking responsibility for why they wound up where they're at!

When you first went looking for the restaurant, let's again pretend you didn't have your cellphone. What could you have done? You could have asked the hotel clerk in the lobby, they may have even given you a map (but let's pretend they didn't). So, you asked the clerk and they gave you verbal instructions as to how to get to the restaurant (and remember, you wanted to walk. You're not taking a cab). So you go outside and start walking the directions that were described to you. You're extremely excited but there were so many instructions that you don't know where to go anymore so you start *asking people* around you. You might find a gas station and ask the people there, or you could even ask people you pass on the sidewalk! You ask for landmarks along with the directions so you have some reference points along your walk. You finally arrive and the meal was absolutely spectacular and you are SO HAPPY that you enjoyed this fabulous meal but also that you got to your destination in a timely manner because you were hungry!

What was different? The second time you were *resourceful*. In the first example when you just walked aimlessly, having no idea where you were going you *still had access to the <u>same</u> resources*, you just didn't use them! Therefore, the only difference in being successful in both circumstances is that you *enlisted* the help from people around you who *knew* where to go and how to get there. In both examples you had a goal, which was getting to the restaurant. In the first example you had absolutely no plan for getting there and tried to do everything yourself instead of asking people who had been there before or who were familiar with the city and the restaurant's location.

Again, the second time you used the resources around you, which meant asking questions, interacting with others and finding out the best route to get to the restaurant. Then you took those directions and applied them to your life with your own unique strut and strutted your way along the path, continually using the resources that were *all around you*. You may have misjudged your direction along the way but it didn't matter to you because it was your first time trying to get there and you knew you had *unlimited resources all around you!*

Which person do you *want* to be? Most of us are like the first person in at least one aspect of our life. We want something so badly but don't actually use the resources all around us. Sometimes we have a destination in mind and don't have a specific word-for-word plan of how we are exactly going to get there. However, simply by asking the right questions our path can become more clear. If we don't ask those questions and wonder why we didn't get to where we wanted to go we're left feeling alone, unmotivated, lost, like things are just never going to work out for me, why me?

The things in your life that you're really great at you've practiced, you've *asked for help*, you've sought advice, you've read articles and books, your plan has started to take shape, and you've taken *action* in order to achieve the goal that you want so badly!

If someone's going on a driving trip across the country and they want to do specific activities in specific areas we would expect that they had a map and a plan. Our lives function in the exact same way. If you want to get somewhere you haven't been before you have to have a plan, you have to be willing to ask for help (use your resources), and you have to be willing to take action and go down roads you may have never been down before. Just imagine the path to your destination is lit by a beautiful sunny day and the path is lined with people who only want to help you along the way. How would that change your feelings toward trying something new?

Another really important word related to planning and taking action is you must make a *commitment*. We have to take a look at our incentives and want to make a change. Or we have to find something that is going to make our resolve and commitment, to what we want to accomplish, concrete.

Who are some of the people in your personal networks, your business networks, your social networks who have been to where you want to go in your life? Make a list. If you're not satisfied then list a few people you know *of* that you could reach out to. There is an endless supply of possible resources to help us along our journey through life. All we have to be willing to do is *commit, act,* and *ask.*

Phase One: Into The Mind

The Discovery of the Two Worlds

Life is born out of struggle. At least that's the way it's perceived. Our opinions, perspectives, and judgments impact our reality and directly affect our experience of reality. Pick any situation and no people will perceive the experience in the exact same way. Perception is as unique as each individual is on this planet.

Our bodies and minds are complex systems that strive to work efficiently and effectively to process information. In our realities, patterns arise and people can relate to one another through patterns and shared experiences, emotions, thoughts, ideas, and passions. People unconsciously categorize their experiences and over time the body and mind become more efficient and effective in eliciting responses to external stimuli *based on* our internal categorization systems.

This can be extremely useful especially when quick responses are necessary or simply in responding to the everyday stimuli that we experience. For example, if our loved one is leaning in for a kiss our response is natural as we move toward that person and reciprocate those feelings. This mechanism can work in other ways, for example, in responding to threats. We don't need to have a threat explained to us because we don't have time to think things through in threatening situations. Our response is automatic.

The areas where this mechanism of judging, labeling, and

defining doesn't necessarily serve us well is when it closes us off from experiencing life more fully. Here's a small example, we'll call it *The Waitress Analogy*. Imagine you walk into a restaurant and see a waitress behind the front desk. Now imagine that within a half a second of seeing her something in your unconscious mind gets triggered and your mind goes on a rampage. Your mind races to judgments and conclusions like *she's a snotty, stuck-up, (insert expletive here), know-it-all, who doesn't even appreciate the fact that she has a job, who doesn't even want to be here, who thinks she's too good to be here*, and you haven't even taken your second step through the doorway! Have you done this before? Or how many times have you done it today? Or worse yet, how many times have you done this and not even been consciously aware that you have because you just end up believing the snap judgments you make in your mind?

How much of a chance have we given the waitress? More interesting though is our interaction with the waitress will not be based on how she's actually feeling, thinking, or being but through our judgment of who we think she is. Our thoughts have no bearing on who the person actually is and are entirely based on our own thoughts of who we think she is. The interesting thing is that our *vibes,* our *energy*, even our *physiology* and our *demeanour* will change with the judgments we've made. People will be able to notice the effects of our judgments through our body language and our communication. This will, in turn, elicit a *reaction* from the waitress based on our unconscious judgments. The result is that our judgment *predetermines* the experience we will have with the waitress.

What are the implications for this scenario? Let's take a step back and determine how we even got to this judgment of this waitress, *we don't even know her!* But something in our unconscious mind is telling us that we do. It's saying we know exactly who this person is. Our unconscious mind will open all of the relevant 'filing cabinets' in our mind and say (and this is happening completely unconsciously, we're not even aware of this process occurring!) we're justified in having these judgments and opinions of this waitress because of this, this, this, and this. What is the this, this, this, and this that set our mind off? What experiences have we had that would allow us to 'pull out' these horrible judgments and project them onto this waitress? Did we get rejected by a girl when we were younger and this waitress happens to remind us of her on an unconscious level? Did someone put an idea inside of our mind when we were younger that would explain our reaction to seeing this waitress? There are infinite possibilities as to why we could be having this unconscious recall and projecting it onto the waitress. Was it the way she looked, her posture, her attire, or her facial expression?

Our minds can be *extremely quick* to make these judgments and our environment and the people within it can be completely helpless to these judgments that we make. What hope does the waitress have of impressing us once we've jumped to these conclusions?

In some instances we might even (in our mind) say, *you know, I'll give her a chance to impress me and change my mind about her but I definitely expect her to be the way I thought.* This may be an unconscious thought that we are entirely unaware of. So, we've made an initial judgment of the waitress (which was made unconsciously) and then 'given her a chance' to prove us wrong (which is still directly linked to our unconscious projection). But we actually expect her to fail and live up to the expectations of who we think she is based on our unconscious and judgmental categorization system and we've done all of this having only one foot in the door.

Now, for the waitress, the same is going on in her head but maybe she didn't see you until you had made all of your judgments. So is she seeing you for who you are? Or has something changed in your body language, demeanour, facial expression, or your *vibe* whereby now she is going to be treating you and responding to you based on the unconscious discernments she's making of you and the judgments that you're making of her. So you see how complex this can get, whereby, in the end *neither one of you is actually treating the other as they really are but based on the unconscious judgments each is continually making and this goes back and forth, each of you continuing to react to one another until both are unhappy and go their separate ways never wanting to see each other again.* What an incredible event has taken place and all because of you taking one step into the restaurant and deciding who the waitress was *before ever giving her a chance to be the person she wants to be. So both of you remain trapped in a world of unconscious judgments that neither can see their way out of and if either of you ever saw each other again these thoughts, feelings, and judgments would be stirred up again. And in the end neither one of you would ever know who the other person really is. If you continue on this path will you ever know who you truly are, while living so unconsciously that you're not aware of the judgments your mind is continually making and expressing in your physical language, body language, facial expressions, and energy?*

Everyone is an open book, if you're reading.

What would have happened in the waitress scenario if you had walked in and not judged? If you had walked in and been aware of your thoughts and feelings but remained open to allow the interaction to unfold naturally. The waitress may have made some unconscious judgments on you but if you maintained your openness, maybe her judgments would dissipate and you would both be able to communicate to each other and learn and understand each other at a level representative of the duration of your interaction.

One person can make a difference. One person's level of consciousness can change people. It can change people's experiences of reality, of themselves, of others, of their abilities, of their skills, of their strengths, of their life.

One person.

There is one thing that our brains have come to love regarding these unconscious judgments that we make. Before I reveal what it is let me say that our verbal judgments come into our reality through our unconscious mind. We don't realize the judgments we make are based on our perception, which stems from our unconscious mind. In addition to making unconscious judgments, we remain unconscious, unaware, and oblivious to their far-reaching effects and impacts on the lives of others as noted in the above waitress example.

The thing that our brains love to do is to categorize and label. This is so that our brains can more easily, more efficiently, and more effectively judge a situation and know how to respond. Just like the waitress example, if we are unconscious when we enter the restaurant, our mind may be set off on determining how it should interact with the people it comes across, and it will search its database of experience and history to determine how it should interact with this person based NOT ON THE PRESENT BUT ON THE PAST. *Because everything stored in our brain is from the past.*

When we judge what we *expect* reality to be like, which, we do unconsciously, guess what... *that is EXACTLY what it BECOMES LIKE!* Said another way,

Our reality becomes what we expect it to be.

Let's review. Our brain likes to be efficient and effective and quick to respond to its environment. Therefore, it categorizes and labels information and stores it in our brain. Then, in the present, it draws upon *historical* and *unconsciously stored* information and applies this, what it *'knows'*, in order to respond or react to the present. So our experience of the present is a reflection of our past judgments that we recall and bring forward to effectively and efficiently communicate with the present situation. Said slightly differently, our present reality is based on historical projections of our unconscious categorizations and labels to interpret the external environment we are experiencing in the present moment.

That's a lot of information.

Basically, are we aware of all of the judgments, categorizations, and labels that we use on a daily basis and what kind of impact do they have on our life and the way we experience it?

From *The Waitress Analogy*, our unconscious, historical projections in the form of labels, judgments, and categorizations impacted our experience with her. Our interaction would have been exactly what we expected based on these categorizations and reactivity in the situation.

The unconscious mind loves to run on loops. It finds this effective and efficient in responding to situations. For example, we judge a situation, we have an experience, it's what we expected, and this reaffirms the unconscious loop in our mind thereby strengthening the loop. In *The Waitress Analogy*, the initial judgments that were made upon seeing the waitress are *feedback loops* and our experience with the waitress is reaffirming and strengthening this feedback loop. Therefore, the next time a scenario, similar to seeing the waitress, presents itself we will react in a very similar manner. The reason is that this feedback loop hasn't been challenged. The loop hasn't been interrupted and when it doesn't get interrupted why would a loop do anything differently?

Unconscious loops are very difficult to interrupt or break because we've spent a *huge* amount of time strengthening them. When we are unconscious we are strengthening these loops every day. This is why it is so difficult for us to change. First, we have to become aware of a loop that is playing in our mind. Then we actually have to *want* to change it. Another challenge is that we usually *want* to change the loop but we don't really fully invest ourselves to do so; we don't *fully commit*.

The labels, categorizations, and judgments that our mind makes are endless. There are also endless ways for loops to form and they can be both positive and negative, which is entirely subjective in terms of how we experience the loops that run in our lives. For example, someone might not think there's a problem with judging the waitress and therefore, might not experience that loop or *think* that they experience anything negative from the loop. The reason why I say *think* is that there are always consequences to our actions.

Even if someone doesn't *think* stealing is wrong there are still ripple effects to have done something like stealing.

When thinking about *The Waitress Analogy* you may say or think, *ya well this was just one incident, so what*? But what if we were doing this hundreds of times per day and completely unaware of the fact that we were doing this? What if our entire experience of reality was similar to the one I presented in our example of the waitress? What would that mean for our experience of reality? When we live through our unconscious projections we can *fall victim* to our experiences in our lives.

The most important aspect of this analogy and these ideas is that there is *hope*! *We can change our experience of reality by altering our awareness and consciousness in each moment that we live.* We can challenge and change these loops that run inside our mind. We can broaden our perspective and change our perception of the world and thereby have our experiences evolve. If we raise our level of awareness and consciousness then we will not fall prey to the feedback loops that unconsciously run inside of our minds. Instead, we will realize that we control our reality not by controlling the situation and manipulating it to our advantage over another but by realizing that we *do have control over our ideas, thoughts, labels, judgments, categorizations, AND (maybe most importantly) EXPECTATIONS* of reality. By remaining open-minded we *CAN* alter our course and experience of reality into something that we actually want to experience and that makes things more enjoyable for ourselves, others close to us, and everyone that we interact with.

Okay, so our ideas, thoughts, labels, judgments, categorizations of the world are filed away in the unconscious mind ready to be recalled based on our present situation. This, in turn, impacts our experience of reality and our expectations for what it will bring. Our mind loves loops and will continue down a 'looped' path unless it is interrupted. By interrupting loops we can raise our level of awareness and consciousness and experience our reality in ways we have never done before. *We can change the course of our life by consciously directing our expectations toward ends THAT WE CONSCIOUSLY INTEND!*

We are so much more powerful than we realize in being able to shape the course of our lives and not fall victim to our unconscious loops. In addition to experiencing reality through the unconscious loops in our minds we haven't considered another aspect; *WE* are a part of our reality. As a result, guess what? Our unconscious mind has even turned on itself!

As mentioned before, our unconscious mind wants to judge, label, and define so that it can understand reality and it uses this same system on *our self*. This, to the great detriment of millions in the world, results in us having limiting, critical, and destructive views of ourselves and what we are capable of!

What this means is that if we remain unconscious and unaware of the ideas, thoughts, labels, judgments, and categorizations that we make of life we also remain unconscious and unaware of how that same unconscious filing system affects our self. We then have certain expectations of our reality and of ourselves and through this process a kind of 'tunnel vision' gets created for our life *and* self. At an unconscious level, we impose limits and barriers as to what we can be and/or experience in life.

What a burden we have to bear! However, because we are so unconscious to these workings of the inner mind we *accept* our reality as it is. We *expect* things to remain as they are. We have the hope that it can change and that we can change but not that we can *actually* achieve it ourselves and we don't seek it out. And by seeking it out I mean seeking it from within ourselves.

Let's consider the following to further our understanding. All we need to do to understand our unconscious beliefs is to start listening to the language we use. For example, making statements that include 'but' and 'however'. Statements that include these words completely negate whatever you said preceding it. Here's an example, *I really want to start working out but...., I really want to lose weight however..., I really want a different job but..., I really want to start going to bed earlier however..., I really want to stop smoking but..., I really want to be more confident but...*, and so forth. Let's come to a realization and understanding about these statements. You actually *don't want these things* because there's a reward you get for not following through. There is *something you receive that is more important to you than receiving whatever it is you say you want before the but or however.*

What's holding you back from making the commitment? Here's the fascinating thing… so I've mentioned that our unconscious mind defines, labels, categorizes, and then files away the result of that experience to draw upon on a later date when something in that present moment triggers that 'filing cabinet' in our mind to be opened and the file within presented to us so that we can better understand our present reality. Okay, so that's what we do but what's the fascinating part?

The fascinating part is that however we unconsciously decide to set up the filing cabinet system and however we unconsciously decide what is and is not relevant becomes important for us because *whatever WE decide is important becomes familiar to us, becomes comfortable to us, feels safe for us, feels secure for us*. Another important fact is that our unconscious mind can be absolutely overpowering and we can really feel truly helpless to its desires. If and when we begin the process of changing our unconscious mind it can represent a very difficult time in our lives, because our conscious mind comes into *direct conflict with* our unconscious mind and they are two opposing worlds and forces. If we are left without support it can be devastating for ourselves, our worlds, our relationships, our careers, and our lives!

We *need* support through this transition.

So our unconscious minds' define, categorize, label, and

'store away experiences' in order to be able to draw upon them quickly when needed to relate to our present reality. Our unconscious is saying, *see how I keep you safe in any circumstance, I help you to quickly define and label what a situation is going to be like so that you can quickly respond and adapt to it. By doing this I help you feel safe and secure and comfortable.* In this way, anything that contradicts an unconscious mind's filing system can be dismissed or we become defensive when our labels, definitions, categorizations, and therefore, our whole filing system, has been challenged. We *take a stand against the injustice of the other person's imposing ideas, will, thoughts, feelings, or the situations experience.* We take this stand and our unconscious mind says *YOU WILL NOT WIN! I KNOW WHO I AM AND WHAT I NEED AND YOU WILL NEVER BE ABLE TO CHALLENGE ME.*

Our unconscious mind, therefore, creates barriers to our full experience of our lives simply because it believes it is doing us justice by 'protecting us'. Our unconscious mind is our primitive mind and it served us so well in our more unconscious ancestors. However, human beings, century over century, have continued to have their conscious minds develop. This aspect of ourselves, this aspect of our mind, is curious, wants to learn, wants to discover, sees no boundaries, sees only possibilities, has no doubts, has no fears, and is full of energy that just wants to be expressed.

The path toward consciousness will not be complete until our unconscious and conscious minds are unified. Until our unconscious minds see that our conscious mind is nothing to actually fear and that if our unconscious mind embraces our conscious mind then that human being can find peace within themselves and will be able to live a life they find meaningful and be able to live out their true life's purpose.

The world of the unconscious mind must be embraced by the conscious mind. The unconscious mind has been around for so long and has helped to shape who we are as individuals and will continue to be a part of us.

The unconscious mind wants to be able to define and label who we are; the conscious mind knows there are no bounds to who we can be.

This quote scares the SH!T out of the unconscious mind and makes it want to shrivel up.

So again, the unconscious mind labels, categorizes, and defines our experiences and the people within it *and* it turns this 'filing cabinet system' upon itself *for even MORE protection*. The unconscious mind labels, categorizes, and defines what we are and are not capable of doing, being, becoming, thinking, and achieving. This creates even more turmoil for the conscious mind who just wants to become someone with all the gifts each of us possess. However, this labeling, categorizing, and defining of ourselves boxes us in, traps us and some of us can't even see that our own subconscious has boxed us in and put a ceiling on what we can achieve.

This is a devastating blow to each human being who sets limits on themselves and therefore, never lives up to who or what they can become in life. When the conscious mind is completely oblivious to the workings of the unconscious mind we can live in fear; we are scared and afraid of everything when really it's a lack of awareness of the box our own mind has placed us in. This *is NOT* anybody's fault and any attempt at blaming a person or a part of a person is simply allowing the conscious and unconscious minds to remain in conflict and disconnected.

There *IS* hope! Everything that has been said doesn't mean that people aren't okay the way that they are. There is always more to learn about each other and ourselves. This also doesn't mean that everyone should be doing any and all activities and that they shouldn't have ones they don't like. Of course there are going to be things that each of us are better at or each of us like better than others do. It doesn't mean that we're not all meant to be doing the jobs that we're doing or be in the relationships we're in or be the size we are. It's simply about starting where we're at and raising our level of awareness and consciousness to improve our lives and enjoyment of them, however we may *consciously* define that for ourselves.

There are parts of ourselves that we deny though. There are parts of our lives that our unconscious mind rules and our conscious mind wants to take back ownership. However, you do have to embrace the unconscious mind and everything that it has given you because if you don't then it will most likely come back to 'haunt you' because you can't run from something that is a part of you!

So what do you do? Are you happy with your life? If so, maybe close the book now. Are you curious about what life has to offer and your role in it and would like to find greater satisfaction? Then you're on the right path. As the saying goes, *seek and you shall find*.

Are you tired of your life being and feeling like a roller coaster that you're not driving? Well, I hate to break it to you but you *are* driving, just not the conscious part of you. Let's go back to those statements that were mentioned before, for example, *I want to lose weight but*. Your conscious mind is stating the first part but your unconscious mind has to get its 'two cents in' and it says everything after and including the but! This is why you are in conflict. This is why you haven't made the commitment to change. This is why you are not confident in making the change. This is why you continue to experience roller coaster results! Your conscious and unconscious minds and their desires are pulling you in *opposing directions*.

When you're going down that roller coaster and losing all that weight your conscious mind is in control and you feel fantastic and proud of yourself. However, if you haven't embraced your unconscious mind and are not aware of its inner workings to keep you the way you are then your conscious mind is *fighting* to stay in the drivers seat but your unconscious mind will overpower your conscious mind, take control of the 'wheel' on the roller coaster and guess where you're going? Right *back up that scale* and there ain't nothing you can do about it because that's how powerful our unconscious mind is. It has *way more* fighting experience than our conscious mind so that's why it's better not to pick a fight with it. *IF* your conscious mind does stay in power maybe for days, weeks, years, decades, or even life, and you haven't embraced your unconscious mind, the whole time your conscious mind is in the driver's seat for this aspect of your life it will feel like it's a fight. It will feel like work. It will be challenging and maybe after a certain amount of time you'll feel okay about everything and maybe your unconscious and conscious mind made amends with one another without you even knowing about it. It could be that *ignorance is bliss.*

You see, when we are *unaware* of these two minds at work within each of us we believe we're making 'conscious' decisions, judgments, labels, categorizations, and definitions as we go through our daily lives. We live within the confines of the unconscious mind's perception of the world, the people in it, and the various situations and circumstances we find ourselves in.

As the famous quote by Anaïs Nin goes, *We don't see the world as it is, we see it as we are.* I'd like to add that our view of the world is perceived through the lens of the unconscious mind, made up of all of its labels, categorizations, definitions, and judgments.

Our unconscious mind has formed this view of the world based on our experiences in it, the majority of which was formed in our most influential years when we were very young. Again, our unconscious mind has done this to protect us, to comfort us, and to keep us safe. The unconscious mind doesn't judge whether something is good or bad necessarily but first and foremost it judges as to whether it keeps us safe. The idea of 'safe' for the unconscious mind is determined by our experiences when we were younger and the things and ideas that were literally *impressed upon* our minds. The unconscious mind can then become leery of the world that is different from its categorizations as to what is safe, familiar, and comfortable.

Another thing that complicates these ideas even more is that just because a person has had a certain perception impressed upon them doesn't mean that their *entire* life will be viewed through that unconscious perception. Let's look at an example. Imagine there's a woman who's extremely successful but she continues to have difficulties in her personal relationships. The reason she has difficulty in her personal relationships is that her unconscious mind has beliefs that conflict with her conscious mind. So, in terms of her successful career it is quite possible that her unconscious and conscious minds are in tune with one another and this enables her to be driven and very successful in her career.

However, thinking back to the relationship issue for this woman, she could consciously want a partner in her life but it could be that her unconscious beliefs about that partner are that they wouldn't be supportive of her, they wouldn't respect her, they wouldn't allow her to be as successful as she would like to be, or any other scenario you can think of. So, the unconscious mind holds a belief about personal relationships that holds this woman back and in order to move forward and find success in her personal relationships she will have to confront her unconscious beliefs, ideas, categorizations, labels, and definitions that her unconscious mind holds in order to experience what she consciously wants to experience in a personal relationship.

Once you unite the conscious and unconscious mind the huge up-and-down roller coaster ride gets smaller or even becomes a straight track. Wouldn't this be a liberating experience for people? To have both their unconscious and conscious minds in complete unison with each other related to weight, related to business, related to relationships, related to physical health, or whatever you would like to work on? I definitely think so!

So where does one begin? In my experience you can try a couple of things. You can try challenging the behaviour. Even though a behaviour is a physical form and our unconscious thoughts are a mental form the results from the changed behaviour could still find their way back to the mental constructs in the mind. Changes in behaviour can result in changes to how we feel and think as we're providing ourselves with new experiences. We would need to have a high level of commitment to change a behaviour because if we haven't raised our level of consciousness our unconscious mind, which doesn't like new things, could be very quick to shut down and stamp out the new experience.

So if behaviour helps raise our level of consciousness then great but if it doesn't we can try something else to challenge our unconscious mental constructs. In order to get to the root of things in the unconscious mind we need to bring greater conscious awareness to the ways in which the unconscious mind likes to exist. There is absolutely no better way to challenge them than with *Questions!* Questions are, by far, the most effective method at exacting change in your life because questions, if asked in an empowering way, can open you up to greater awareness and experience. We'll go over questions more in the next section.

One more analogy before we move to the next phase. This is definitely one of my most favourite analogies and I thought of it a couple of weeks before writing this book while I was running with a friend. This is *The Typecasting Analogy*. Let's start with a definition of the word *typecasting*. When I think of typecasting the first thing I think of is movies and the roles that actresses and actors get *typecasted* to play. For example, you might think of Will Ferrell, who, if he wasn't in a comedy it might feel strange that he's not making people laugh. You might think of Liam Neeson, who, if was in a romantic comedy and not breaking anybody's neck you might get the feeling that 'this just doesn't feel right'. Then there's Dwayne Johnson, who, if he's not in an action thriller and taking his shirt off so you can see his ripped physique then it would just feel like it's not a movie he's supposed to be in...Oh wait, what about the 'Tooth Fairy'? There are exceptions but it still doesn't change the fact that when an actor or actress gets cast for a role they don't usually play it becomes difficult for the audience to relate to the character being portrayed if its just so far from the roles the actor or actress normally play.

Great. Typecasting. But what does that mean for us? We're not actresses or actors going through our lives. Or are we? You see if the unconscious mind is leading the way that we live then we might not be playing the role we want to in the movie of our lives. We may be living out the role of our unconscious mind's definitions, labels, categorizations, and judgments that limit our perception of the world and therefore, our experience of it. The unconscious mind, as it jumps to conclusions about others and our experiences of the world, also possesses filing cabinets of categorizations, judgments, labels, and definitions that represent our beliefs about ourselves. Think of what a burden this could be *and IS* for people. Our unconscious mind doesn't set out to judge the world and not itself. Our unconscious mind wants to be able to know who we are and therefore it casts unconscious labels and definitions upon ourselves.

This inevitably impacts the people that we are in our lives and the *roles* that we play within the movies of our lives. What happens is exactly what happens in the movies with the actors and actresses who get 'typecasted'. Not only do we label and 'typecast' ourselves but *other people typecast us too!* Just as the audience and the filmmakers typecast certain actresses and actors, our friends, family, co-workers, doctors, employers, etc. *TYPECAST US!* The way we have been living our lives is comfortable for people. They 'know what to expect' when they know the role you play in the movie of your life. They've got you labeled and typecasted in their unconscious mind's filing cabinet system.

Their unconscious mind, just like ours, will label, categorize, define, and judge who we are and the role that we play in *their mind*. For anyone trying to 'tackle' their unconscious mind and live more consciously free they will inevitably and naturally change certain 'roles' they play in their life. This is not necessarily an easy task to do on the level of the individual but what can make it even more challenging is the fact that they have to *overcome* the typecasted role they play in the unconscious minds of those closest to them and *THIS* can be the real challenge. Now you don't just have to 'convince' yourself of the new role you're going to play but you have to convince everyone around you who already 'knows who you are'.

This book is about breaking through those typecasted views of ourselves and those we hold over others so that we can be and explore our full potential without any self-imposed limits from our unconscious mind who's really just trying to protect us. We need to protect ourselves less and break through those walls our unconscious mind has set for us and give freedom to our conscious mind to allow it to create all that it is capable of creating in and for our lives!

Now that the initial phase is complete and we understand the mind, we can move on to the next phase. This next phase is the Four C Process, or The Cs To Sow To See as I like to think of it. Contained herein are words that obviously begin with C and if you follow their true wisdom you will be able to live more consciously and live the life that *you consciously* choose, never to be held back again!

These Cs are not rocket science. What's better is that we've *all* applied them in our lives in areas that we are extremely competent in. We *already understand* the process we just haven't been consciously aware of what that process is! All we need to do is apply them in the areas that we *actually want* to change and are *actually committed* to change. I truly hope you enjoy!

Phase Two: The Cs To Sow To See: The Four C Process

The Primary Cs

1.1 Curiosity

Curiosity is akin to the fire inside each and every one of us that propels us forward in our lives. It is a gift that everyone receives or possesses, however, the majority of humanity forgets this innate aspect of our human nature as we grow up and become a part of, or a cog in, mainstream society.

Curiosity is how life begins. Really though, this is how life begins. As kids we begin by exploring, being open to our surroundings, and curious about everything around us and how it all works. Everything is exciting and interesting to us. We're absolutely amazed by life and we are so incredibly open to all it has to offer. Don't believe this? Watch any child play and imagine (and I don't mean on their iPod, iPad, iPhone, or computer!). Children are amazing because they are curious about themselves and the people and things in their surroundings. They want to discover, learn, feel, touch, play, and shape their reality and experience in any way possible.

Said another way, they are curious about their realities but can also imagine their realities. These innate abilities seem so simple yet, in actuality, are so tremendously important and complex. Curiosity directed toward your strengths and passions has the potential to make absolutely any person successful in their lives. Curiosity, mixed with imagination, has the potential to lead people to continually uncover, discover, understand, and see new truths about their reality. If we consider anyone who's become successful in their professional lives, which may include starting or running a business, these characteristics are deeply ingrained within their entire being.

So what happens to the rest of us? How do we become disconnected from the infinite potential that comes with curiosity and imagination? The world is filled with powerful distractors that detract curiosity and imagination from our realities.

There are people who never lose their curiosity in business, in their career, in their relationships, in the arts, in their hobbies, in their books, and so forth. However, one thing that successful people will do is hone this quality, this characteristic and ensure it is specifically directed towards their goals in life. Think about it, if you're not curious as to how you can create, improve, learn, discover, achieve, grow, etc. what kind of motivation, if any, are you going to have to work towards achieving a goal? For example, if it's a business venture they'll focus their creative and curious energies on their ideas and their business as they formulate ways of imagining, creating, or improving anything related to their business.

Curiosity is the key first step in life. If we're lucky it was an integral part of the way that we were raised, and this characteristic was fostered and developed within us. If this was the case then curiosity has become a part of our daily lives and is something that has never been forgotten within us and is something we can turn to in our lives to discover ways to make our lives better. It's also a characteristic that will help keep us young at heart. I have a saying that I've really grown to like; *I will always be youthful because I'm young at heart.*

I think curiosity, by its nature, has an innocent childlike quality to it that is so important as we move through life. Don't mistake this quality as something that is immature, naive, and weak. It is absolutely, and tremendously, powerful and it does have the potential and the strength to transform our lives and our realities. If we remain curious we will resist the tendency to become hardened by reality and experience. If you are curious you will be open to life as it unfolds and will be better able to adapt to all of the change that is inevitable as we move through life.

Curiosity simultaneously asks a question and seeks an answer.

To me curiosity implies an openness to experience; an openness to life. It does not close itself off from the endless possibilities that exist outside of a specific question. A state of curiosity moves us beyond generalizations, assumptions, expectations, labels, definitions, and categorizations (which limit our experience) and into a realm of truly endless possibilities. Curiosity moves us from dwelling in the unconscious mind to existing and creating with the conscious mind. Therefore, with curiosity we possess the power to break down the barriers of the unconscious mind. Nothing can stand in our way if we choose to live with curiosity. But we must choose.

As I mentioned at the beginning, curiosity is that fire inside of us, that light, that energy, that always lives within us, waiting to be re-realized as our social coronation requires we neglect and/or completely abandon this notion to serve, not the purposes within ourselves, but the agendas of others. So, let's focus on the fire. What we can say about a fire?

Fire lights the way.

The Bonfire Analogy. Think of a large bonfire at night burning through a vast, expansive land. If you're off in the distance and within sight, you can always find your way back to the fire and its' warmth and the energy that is alive within it. Curiosity is the fire ablaze in each of us. It's there, we've just veered further and further away that we've forgotten it was right there within us all along. Our unconscious mind has helped us stray from the fire within us.

What do fires need? Fires need fuel (wood), oxygen, and heat. How do these relate to the fire inside of all of us? Oxygen is akin to our dreams, the things we focus on in life, our sense of appreciation for life, our visualizations about our lives and what we want them to become. The wood/fuel is the physicality that we make out of our dreams, the actions we take, and the interactions we create. Heat is the curiosity that exists within our spirit and the *energy* that comes from this source. Each aspect, the intangible oxygen (our dreams and visions), the physical fuel (taking action), and heat (our curious spirit) is essential to keeping the fire alive and burning brightly within ourselves.

Where and when we have curiosity we have *passion* and we find *inspiration*. Curiosity exists in the conscious mind; the mind that knows no boundaries. When we are born our conscious mind is absolutely free to live, breathe, and create. Our unconscious mind develops over time based on our experiences, environment, and the people within it. If the unconscious mind is continually strengthened then this draws us away from our conscious mind and the curiosity that exists within it.

How do we reignite the fire of curiosity within ourselves? Firstly, and most importantly, follow your passions, your interests, and the things that you could do endlessly and receive so much joy, happiness, and satisfaction from. Reconnecting with your passions will help you rediscover the fire inside of you. These underutilized passions within us are our inspirations, our motivations, and our energy. Secondly, develop an understanding of the language that you use because this reflects your deeply held beliefs, or the beliefs of your unconscious mind. You begin to develop this understanding by asking yourself questions that are empowering and open-ended.

Questions, if used well, can open us up to possibility. When used in this way we do not need to have a current answer to the thing we want or need. Here are examples of questions that are completely disempowering and will make you feel like a victim of your reality and have no hope or choice to create anything in it. *Why does this always happen to me? Why can't I just find the right person to be with for the rest of my life? Why do I always fail at losing weight? Why can't I find a better job?* These questions presuppose that you will fail and whenever you ask questions like this you will find only failure because that is what you're actually focused on. Your unconscious mind has a tight grasp on that aspect of your reality and although your conscious mind wants to change things for yourself it is not yet aware of this tight grasp the unconscious mind has. The conscious and unconscious minds are in conflict with one another. In order to challenge your unconscious mind and open yourself up to the infinite possibility that exists in each and every moment you must ask empowering questions that presuppose your success. Here are some examples of hopeful, open-ended, and empowering questions. *How <u>will</u> I respond in a dignified, confident, and empowered manner? How <u>will</u> I broaden my perspective <u>even more</u> so that I recognize the opportunities all around me <u>right now</u>? How <u>will</u> I choose strategies that will energize my spirit, satiate my body, and cleanse my mind <u>right now</u>?*

These don't have to necessarily be the questions that you use but do you notice the difference between the first set of questions and the second set of questions? How did they make you feel? Did the second set make you feel open to possibility? Did they make you feel empowered? Did they make you feel a little scared? They may have and the reason for this is that by asking open, inviting, and empowering questions you are bringing the unconscious to light. It would much rather stay hidden and remain unchallenged so it is very possible that you will be met with a sense of discomfort or doubt by asking questions like those in the second set.

In addition, the unconscious mind likes to place things in its filing cabinet system. How would it place an empowering, open, and inviting question within its system of categorization? It's not possible for the unconscious mind to do that because it needs something finite, something defined; *it <u>needs</u> an <u>answer</u>!* But these empowering questions don't necessarily imply an immediate answer, they invite it in! So keep asking them! Over and over! All day! First thing when you wake up, when you brush your teeth, when you're making your bed, when you're going to work, when you're at work, when you're going home, when you're going to the gym, before you go into meetings, after you go to meetings, while you're making dinner, before you go to bed. Write them down, over and over, post them in and around your house, your car, your office, so that you are continually reminded of the power that you possess simply by asking that empowering question!

When creating your own questions use words like *will, even more,* and *right now*. Use words in the present tense. Here's a word of caution and this is extremely important. When you start asking empowering questions this is what will happen to you. You *will* receive an answer. You *will*. Your conscious mind will receive it and *almost as soon as you do the unconscious mind will <u>jump in</u>* and it will throw doubt after doubt after doubt at you and into your mind so that you just brush off the idea and you keep waiting for the 'right' answer! We need to be better listeners so we can hear the answers we seek. When you hear the solutions act on them *immediately*! *Don't wait and don't hesitate*!

The questions we ask ourselves come in two types. Those that reinforce helplessness and those that inspire, empower and make you want to take action! Make sure you're asking the latter!

1.2 Cultivation

So you want to change a certain aspect or many aspects of your life. Step one, you become curious about yourself, how you may be closing yourself off to seeing, feeling, and experiencing things differently through your limiting beliefs and language stemming from the unconscious mind. You see the value in being curious and how this quality is inextricably linked to the idea of being open and when you're open in a situation you are more capable of receiving that which you seek.

Cultivation begins now. Curiosity *is* the fire and you *sense* and *feel* a fire has been lit and you've found a new source of energy that just makes you want to move. You must cultivate this idea of curiosity. You must seek out ways to learn, ways to grow, and you must become more conscious of the language you use with yourself and with others. Cultivation is about developing your abilities, skills, strengths, interests, and passions. At the same time, you continue to ask more empowering and uplifting questions about yourself and your life. The ideas start flowing to you and you become more determined to continue on this new path.

Cultivation is more than asking questions though, it's about practice and taking action. In order to learn something new you must practice it. If you choose not to practice you won't, more fully, learn and understand that which made you curious and intrigued. Cultivation is not something that should ever cease at a certain age.

The act of striving to acquire and develop new skills, ideas, insights, experiences, and relationships should continue throughout our lives. This is what children do so well. They are not deterred; they are determined to continue on a certain path, whether it's in an activity, a situation, or a game.

This quality is absolutely essential to our success as individuals, whether it's in our relationships, our business, our health, or whatever we want to improve. It is a quality whereby, once we allow new things into our lives through curiosity, we develop these ideas and they take more physical forms. By this I basically mean that we take our questions and are then turning them into actions, behaviours, and habits. In addition, if we nurture our curiosity through cultivation then we give both our curiosity and our cultivation the room and space that it needs to continually grow. Ideas that we become naturally curious about and naturally inclined toward are meant to be explored; the conscious mind strives for this.

Let's talk about *failure*. *Failure* only exists in the eye of the beholder. I see 'failure' as a chance or an opportunity to experience, to learn, and to grow. In entrepreneurial endeavours and business, there is so much discussed about how important *failure* is in order to succeed. However, business, just as in life, is a *process*. Here, again, we find language to be of such great importance. Speaking of something as having failed has a negative connotation. If we're in the process of being more conscious of our language and the possibilities and opportunities for our lives we need to use language more constructively and think about things differently.

Life is a process, not an endpoint.

What makes entrepreneurs, or people in general, successful is their ability to cultivate their thoughts, their ideas, their relationships, their experiences, and their skills into something greater in order to change, enhance, or improve their lives and others. Each 'new', positively cultivated skill helps shape or form the foundation for the next one. Nobody learns everything all at once. It's a process and you must cultivate and build off of each preceding idea, thought, skill, action, behaviour, etc. I say 'new' because things simply organically reveal themselves from where we are or have left off. Failure isn't an endpoint, it signifies, highlights, or reveals a new direction that should or could be cultivated and explored.

1.3 Confidence

Can you see the progression here? When a person moves from being curious about something and from there they begin to cultivate and develop that skill, what happens next or through this process? The person naturally becomes more confident. Take a young child for example, they can't walk at first but by watching everyone else around them walk they strive to be capable of doing the same. So what do they do? They certainly don't just get up and walk. It's a process.

Infants are naturally curious and they are definitely curious about all of the things that people around them are doing. They are determined to walk. So, infants will move their limbs, they'll start getting 'tummy time'. As their neck and limbs get stronger they'll start to lift their head up, then they'll be able to get into a crawling position, then they'll be able to crawl. At some point they'll be sitting, then standing with support, then walking with support, then they'll walk on their own, and then, as they say, *you're in trouble.*

Another thing happens, which is slightly off topic but I'll mention it here because we're talking about children. Children are judged their entire life. Parents, doctors, teachers, daycare providers, coaches, etc. all judge 'where the kid is at' in terms of meeting their 'milestones'. Is this of benefit to the child? Or do we start paying too much attention to the checklist of milestones and stop paying attention to the child right in front of us? This is a perfect example of the unconscious mind of others imposing itself on another human being, in this case a child. In this circumstance, our expectations, based on the milestone checklist, have nothing to actually do with *who* the child is but whether they're 'meeting expectations'. So, in terms of understanding *who the child is* does this set a child up for potential failure if they start not meeting certain aspects of the checklist? If this happens the child will then get judged based on an idealistic yet unrealistic milestone checklist *because no two people are the same!* And yet we have this checklist to what? To see if the child is perfect or close to it? What are they if they don't meet all of the items on the checklist in the 'right' amount of time? Are they then deemed a failure? Do we then call them *delayed*?

So we judge children's performance and by judging them, are our words, doubts, labels, expectations, and limits that *we impose on them* beneficial to them or do they have the potential to hold our children back? If, with this topic you're feeling a defensiveness arise within, what would happen if you turned that into curiosity? Remember the unconscious mind *does NOT like to be challenged.* Regardless, in the end I do believe that this area needs much more curiosity to understand the implications of our actions and the beliefs and expectations we place *on* children who are otherwise helpless to the impressions we impose on them.

Let's get back to the children walking though. They've progressed, as discussed, to the point where they can now walk. An important point to note is that confidence is *not* just developed in the end! Every child who walks *develops confidence through the WHOLE process*. Therefore, curiosity, cultivation, and confidence can be occurring somewhat simultaneously.

For the child who walks it is not the endpoint. There is no endpoint. They'll run and play sports, and walking will continue to take them places for their *entire life*. There may become a time where, as the child ages, that they've achieved such confidence in their walking that they take it for granted. It's become second nature. They don't need to think about walking but we definitely still have confidence in walking. Now someone might think that's a silly statement to make but it's true! I don't think we appreciate these accomplishments that we've made in our young lives. We never gave up, we were focused, determined, growing with confidence with each step, going beyond our 'comfort' zone, and stretching our limits.

Wouldn't it be nice to live everyday like we were our toddler self who was going to stop at nothing to walk. Wouldn't it be useful and incredible to take these characteristics that we *all* possess because we've all mastered walking (and/or something similar to it) and apply it to our lives every single day in everything that we do? What would that feel like? Would that feel absolutely incredible?! I know that's the way I want to feel every, single day!

We're confident in so many different ways in our life. We just tend to overlook those areas because they come naturally to us now. But they only come naturally to us because we've been curious, we've cultivated, and we've grown in confidence, over and over and over again in countless ways in our lives to this point in time!

It may seem that curiosity and confidence oppose each other to a certain extent. Curiosity reflects our openness to the world and to the possibility of differing opinions, thoughts, ideas, qualities, people, experiences, and both discovered truths and unsolved mysteries. On the other hand, there is confidence, which implies a certain level of decisiveness, experience, perspective, and knowledge of the way things are and exist. However, confidence is more about knowledge and understanding based on your level of experience or your intuitive nature toward some situation or experience.

Confidence is not as much knowing as it is understanding the process; seeing things from a broadened perspective from having already done so much cultivating to get to the point they've currently reached. Again it is about the process and not an end point.

Confidence speaks to one's belief in one's own abilities and/or knowledge and feelings toward oneself in relation to the environment. When a person is confident, they are able to recognize the qualities and characteristics that are their strengths and also their weaknesses. The confident person realizes that their strengths and weaknesses are neither good nor bad but that they simply exist and are a part of who they are.

1.4 Collaboration

The process would not be complete without the fourth C; *collaboration*. We are *social beings*. Our greatest successes can be multiplied exponentially by working and being with others. We rely on one another. This piece (collaboration) is possibly the most important one because if we don't connect our curiosity, cultivation, and confidence to others then we remain disconnected and unable to share our gifts, talents, experiences, understandings, knowledge, techniques, and so forth with others and the world.

Whether in our personal lives, our relationships, our interests, or our hobbies, life is better when working with others, sharing experiences with others, and collaborating with others. The same goes for business. Collaboration in business is absolutely essential. Even if you're a one- person entrepreneur, your piece of collaboration is with clients, prospects, other experts in the field, etc. We cannot remain devoid of working with others and still find success.

Think about it, when something exciting happens in your life or in your business what is most likely one of the first things you want to do? You want to tell someone else. You're so excited, happy, relieved, or whatever the feeling is and you want to see someone you know, talk to them, or text them so that you can share the experience with them. Collaboration can heighten the level of the energy of an experience or of a team.

Collaboration is an enhancer. It's where you get to see all your hard work come to fruition. You've been curious, you've cultivated, you've become more confident and now you are getting out there and into the world to share those gifts, which you've developed so well and worked so hard on, with the world.

You look at anybody who's successful in one or many aspects of their life and these Four Cs *will definitely* be a part of their approach to their success. They may not have ever thought of them in this way but they will be there. There is *no way* for someone to develop success without going through this Four C Process. Now, this process is not linear. You *can* think of it as cyclical, which would proceed from curiosity to cultivation to confidence to collaboration and back to curiosity again. However, you may start being curious, move into cultivation but upon beginning to practice new curiosities are forming and you could revisit that. Regardless of *how* you proceed, the fact remains that the Four C Process is a surefire way to succeed. The Four Cs feed off one another and build off one another.

Through working the Four C Process in a certain area in your life you recognize a natural energy source that is present within you. It's always been there but maybe you haven't noticed it, however, with this process you will reignite that energy source within you. You will reunite the unconscious and conscious mind and your life will be more aligned to your purpose as you've taken the time to develop it.

Just as exercise is important for our physical body this process will feel like exercise for your mind. It won't necessarily come naturally to you at first, just like walking didn't come naturally to you at first when you were an infant. Through practice and continually taking your mind and body through the Four C Process, related to something that *you care deeply about,* you will find peace, excitement, and success within and for yourself.

The Secondary Cs: The Supporting Cast & Crew

We've reviewed the primary Cs of the Four C Process, which are absolutely essential for success. The following Cs represent the supporting cast. The majority of the following Cs are factors that you definitely want to ensure are a part of your process toward success, while others are ones to be cautious of.

2.1 Consistency

Consistency is absolutely mandatory in life, that is, if you're aiming to be successful in a given area. Your results stem from actions that you repeat, over and over. Consistent actions lead to habits and if you're less than thrilled with some of the habits that *you've* created then you are *definitely* going to have to take some consistent action in order to change the results that you are currently receiving.

I love sports and if you look at any of the professionals who are at the top of their game they are practicing *consistently* day in and day out. Have you ever been working out consistently and then taken a break for a bit? Maybe you went on vacation and didn't workout or maybe you were sick or injured. How did it feel when you went back to working out? The things you were doing with ease days or weeks before can seem like a challenge especially if you're coming back from an injury or sickness.

In order to achieve lasting change in our lives we must be consistent. If we want to change the unconscious mind's hold over our conscious mind then we must consistently exercise the Four Cs so that we can wear down the unconscious mind and let it see the light that the conscious mind has to offer!

2.2 Challenge

Challenge. The process of change, if its path and process is maintained, will challenge you to your core. You've probably heard the quote:

Life begins at the end of your comfort zone.
Neale Donald Walsch

The task of seeking better of and from yourself is not a simple one. It is one that will leave you feeling challenged on an ongoing basis. It is 'the path less traveled'. This is why some succeed and others do not. It is a challenge to look deeply and inquisitively into oneself and reflect on how you've been living your life and what you want to change. The challenge is also starting that journey toward what you want from your life.

I think some of us expect that someone is going to come along and save us from the life we're leading and that there will be no challenge, we'll just magically become what we want and have everything that we want. I hate to break it to you but you're going to have to work and literally the biggest obstacle in obtaining greater success in your life is *you*.

2.3 Conflict

This is a C to be wary of. Whether conflict is positive or negative all depends on how it is managed. Conflict exists both internally within ourselves and externally as we are social beings and when our ideas are shared they go up against another individual's perception of that same idea. The potential result? Conflict.

Conflict can be well managed provided we've paid close attention to the Four C Process. For example, if we've established a strong relationship with another person through the Four C Process we would have developed rapport, mutual respect and understanding between one another. In this instance, if our opinions or ideas differed from one another they would be more readily accepted and openly discussed because we would be working through the conversation with our conscious minds, which keeps us naturally more open to experience because our conscious minds just want to learn and grow.

I've always viewed conflict as an *opportunity for growth*. If both individuals manage conflict through their conscious minds then they will definitely have a chance to experience that growth. If that is the case then differing opinions or ideas will be able to be accepted and discussed more freely and openly than if there wasn't that strong relationship.

People's perceptions are personal; they have the potential to be tied to an individual's personality or their unconscious mind.

Some people have developed that way. When an idea is attached to someone's identity, (and this is almost always on an unconscious level) anything that is counter to this unconscious and tightly held idea feels, to the person, like it's an attack on them as a person. The result is defensiveness and good luck trying to have an open, honest, and understanding conversation with that person! I think, at least at some point in our lives, we can think back to a time where we've been defensive.

A defensive individual may be willing to share their ideas about their perceptions with you but they are less likely to want to hear what you have to say if it contradicts what they said and believe based on their unconscious mind's filing cabinet system. The reason for this, again, is the idea is attached to their personality or identity. This defensive person exemplifies an individual who is not consciously aware of their biases or perceptions and the concrete attachment to these that exists within them. Any attempt at getting them to see things otherwise will more than likely fail, at least if you take a direct approach.

There *is* hope though! If a successful approach were to be made with a defensive individual it would have to be indirect so that the individual didn't foresee the place you were leading them to. One gentle way of confronting a defensive person is through analogies or stories. So you end up telling the person a story that completely relates to their behaviour or perception and by them hearing this story about this 'other person' (really it's about *them!*) they come to some realization about themselves.

Here's *The Scare Analogy* to demonstrate this idea. Let's say you're trying to scare someone. They're standing right in front of you and you say, *BOO!* They'll think something is wrong with you if you try and scare them while standing right in front of them and it's never going to work. The person's quick response is representative of the unconscious mind; it's always on the lookout and this kind of direct approach will run into the 'brick wall' that is the unconscious mind. If you attack from directly in front of the person the unconscious mind will be very much aware and will defend the attack flawlessly. They'll just end up putting up more walls and you may never have the opportunity to approach them again about this specific topic or area that you'd like them to gather more insight into.

Here's scenario two. Let's say instead of you trying to scare them while standing right in front of them you've teamed up with someone else. So, while you're distracting the person from the front (just by talking to them), the other person sneaks up behind them and scares the heck out of them! There, it worked! This is an indirect approach to effectively infiltrate unconscious mind's fortress around the person you scared. This tactic gets around the conflict that would arise from directly confronting the unconscious mind. In this analogy, you're still you and the 'person' you've teamed up with to scare your friend is the analogy itself.

Okay, so what do I mean? To confront the unconscious mind

it helps to do so in various ways. I mentioned before that when your conscious mind has an idea about doing something new and exciting for yourself your unconscious mind can be quick to stamp out that idea. So one key would be to act *really really quickly on that initial thought before your unconscious mind has a chance to deter you!* This method can be really effective. For example, your thought is, I want to start working out and before you finish that thought you *get out of the house and go do something as quickly as possible before your unconscious mind even knows what's happening.* This is equivalent to 'scaring' a person. You take action before the person even knows what's happening.

Another method would be you reading and learning about subjects that your conscious mind wants to explore, and is curious about, that are going to help you move toward the goals that you have for your life. This will begin the Four C Process and will slowly chip away at the unconscious mind's grasp that it has on you.

A third method is analogies, comparisons, examples, and reflections. This is so effective because it takes your mind on a journey that isn't 'directly' about yourself but actually relates specifically to yourself. Analogies, along with increasing your awareness about something, offer a different vantage point from which to view and experience life, or a certain situation, or a certain emotion, etc. This is exactly the indirect approach we need so that the conscious mind can recognize and see the unconscious mind at work. An analogy is like taking yourself on a really nice and interesting ride and then at the end of it holding up a mirror to your face and then saying, *See! It was YOU who we were talking about the whole time!* This scares the heck out of the unconscious mind and the conscious mind takes note of this. The conscious mind gets an opportunity to notice the unconscious mind's ways and reactions. In addition, analogies will help to kick start the Four C Process especially if it's an intriguing, interesting, and deep analogy that gets you thinking. Because when you get thinking you might get curious and if you get curious you start asking questions and you start learning and then you're well on your way in the Four C Process to changing any aspect of your life.

On the journey through life you will inevitably find conflict. Once you become fascinated and curious about the conflict that exists within yourself and between others, and recognize the ways of the unconscious mind, and then begin to shift the strength to the conscious mind, everything becomes easier and more manageable. It feels as if nothing can stand in your way. And that's becaues now *you're out of your own way!*

2.4 Check-Ins

Checking in with yourself is such a great strategy to build upon. How do you know where you stand, how you feel, or what you're thinking if you're not checking in with yourself? Checking in with yourself is a great way to get your conscious mind active and in tune with what's going on around you and inside you. With practice your conscious mind will become better at noticing what the unconscious mind is doing and if and how it's getting in your way of accomplishing things you want to.

This is important as it is a way to bridge our unconscious and conscious minds in order to raise our level of consciousness and live in a manner that reflects our highest self.

Becoming more in-tune with yourself is something that everyone should strive for and once you exercise the 'check-in' muscle more and more it becomes more natural (just like anything you do over and over!). This is where practices like meditation, breathing, yoga, and other similar practices or variations of them might be helpful to bring greater awareness to yourself, your emotions, and the way you're feeling.

Your unconscious mind can sometimes (or more often for others!) run in loops. They could be loops of stress, anxiety, depression, super energy, happiness, passion, or anything you can think of. These loops could be running more than we actually realize at times too and it can be dizzying if we get carried away with them.

We can get swept up into the whirlwind of the mind and then get lost and can't seem to find our way out.

When first beginning any kind of spiritual practice we may notice these loops more often because we're turning off outside distractions and just listening to what's going on inside. Then we're like, WHOA, and say, *I can't stand practicing meditation because all I can hear is my thoughts and they're driving me insane!* All of these thoughts are the unconscious mind at work and it doesn't like to stop because it hasn't had to in such a long time because we avoid facing it! Practicing meditation involves bringing the conscious mind's attention to a higher level of consciousness and that allows us to lower or turn off the volume of the unconscious mind.

Here's an idea of how we can think of the unconscious loops that run inside our unconscious minds. We'll call it *The Train Analogy*. Imagine your unconscious thoughts are a train going around a circular loop. Most of the time we're *ON* the train. We are swept up by our whirlwind thoughts and can't find a way *off* the train. Now let's imagine there's a bridge that goes over top of the train tracks. Imagine the train slows down just enough so that you can get off the train. You walk up the steps on the bridge and now you're on top of the bridge. Once you get up there you're going to watch the train (your thoughts) as it does continuous loops in a circular pattern that you can see entirely from the bridge where you are. Now remember, the *you* on the bridge represents your conscious mind and the unconscious mind is represented by the train. While you're on top of the bridge you're going to watch and observe your thoughts and because *you* are your conscious mind you're going to do this in a nonjudgmental way. You're going to do this with fascination! You're going to do this with curiosity! Just watch and observe as they go around and around. It's fascinating to watch them go. Maybe the train eventually slows and then you're attention is drawn to the scene beyond the track and you venture out there into the wonderfully peaceful space that exists all around that train track that we just didn't take notice of before. You breathe deeply and your body relaxes and your mind finds peace.

    This is an analogy you could definitely practice if you felt inclined and see what peaceful places and journeys you get taken to once you take notice of the beauty that exists outside of your unconscious loops. Remember to check-in with your mind regularly no matter where you are during each day; that is, have your conscious mind check-in with unconscious mind in order to remain open and curious as to what it may notice around you and within you.

2.5 Contemplation

Contemplation relates really nicely to checking-in. I wanted to mention it separately to drive home a point. If you've ever tried to meditate, focus on your breathing, or even in yoga you may notice how difficult it is to shut off your mind. That's the unconscious mind and you're actually tuning in to the stream that plays continuously in the background (in your unconscious mind) for our entire lives. Practicing meditation, yoga, and breathing allows us to tap into that stream of unconsciousness to raise our level of consciousness so that we can't even hear the stream anymore. We raise ourselves above it. The stream is still there when we return but it has less power in determining what we do in our lives because we've risen above it and give less power to it.

Another important concept that relates to contemplation and our continuous unconscious stream is dwelling on situations, choices, thoughts, actions, or anything that we've done, thought, or seen. The mind is a great recorder and will play back things over and over for us to relive in any moment that we want. Like I mentioned earlier, we have filing cabinets upon filing cabinets within our minds that our unconscious will gladly pull out anytime that we want and we can replay moments on repeat over and over and over and over and over. You get the picture.

Even one small incident can trigger a stream of unconsciousness that seems unstoppable. Here's *The Coffee Shop*

Analogy. You decide to smile at an attractive woman at a coffee shop and she makes a slightly disgusted face. Within the span of 5 seconds you've thought, *what did I do? Do I have something in my teeth? Is there something wrong with my hair? Why doesn't she like me? Did I do something wrong? I was just trying to be friendly. Oh, this always happens to me. I'm just trying to meet a nice girl. Why doesn't anybody like me? What's wrong with me? I'm going to be lonely forever.* You put your head down and start to sulk. Then a guy comes from behind you, walks by and over to the woman's table, and sits down. You realize that he had been in line behind you and she had made the face in response to something he had done behind you and that she hadn't even noticed your smile!

Do you see how we can torture ourselves over little things? The thoughts that we had in this analogy go away momentarily. They arose out of our unconscious mind's filing cabinets. This scenario only served to strengthen our unconscious beliefs that were exposed. These thoughts and feelings *will* come up again unless we bring more consciousness to these moments and challenge the *unconscious* thought processes behind them. How many assumptions were made in that split second when the smile wasn't reciprocated? If this resonates with you it's time to bring greater consciousness to our unconscious thought patterns and stop them dead in their tracks! Who's with me?!

Contemplation and curiosity are important in learning more about these processes. Stay open minded and nonjudgmental and just allow these unconscious thoughts to arise and then fall away. Notice them happening but don't believe them. Don't give them any weight or value!

2.6 Criticism

This is one to be wary of and our unconscious minds are an absolute master at it. It can be like your conscious mind sees your unconscious mind and tries to escape but then the unconscious mind's trusty friend, *criticism*, comes out of nowhere, grabs you, and body slams you to the ground. If you try to run away from *criticism* you have no hope. It will hunt you down and find you and bring you right back to living within and under the unconscious mind's reign.

It's a very fine line to be constructively critical and yet nonjudgmental. Becoming critical and judgmental is our primitive mentality of the unconscious mind; one that pushes the ceiling back over ourselves and limits our potential to get out of the place we are in. Reflecting in a constructively critical and nonjudgmental way opens up the sky and the possibilities for ourselves become limitless. It is a liberating feeling to have this occur.

The ego, or unconscious mind, uses its trickery and judgmental tones to close ourselves off. We say things like 'I can't, I won't, its impossible', etc. We become stuck in emotional states and fester in them in a cloud of negativity. We hate these times in our lives but there is a part of us that loves them. This is a familiar place. No matter how negative of a place it is, it is home to ourselves at this point in our lives and our unconscious mind loves it. It basks in this. It bathes in this. There's an emotional attachment to these places. Many people remain unaware of their ability to free themselves from these critical states, loops, or patterns.

Be curious about criticisms, judgments, and conclusions that you jump to because it is most likely the unconscious mind at work and working very effectively and efficiently at keeping you prisoner. Start by asking questions, get curious about the conclusions, judgments, and criticisms that you have especially if they're being held over someone else or even yourself. When we hold criticisms over another person we undoubtedly hold them over ourselves, otherwise we wouldn't have them!

Be reflective, be curious, be fascinated by the criticisms that we come up with and learn about them. Bring your consciousness to the unconsciousness of them.

2.7 Communication

If you haven't already understood how important communication is in our overall physical, mental, emotional, and spiritual health and our overall place in the world, let me reiterate its importance here. What we put out into the world comes back to us. When we communicate unconsciously and then wonder why we are where we are we need to develop greater consciousness about what we are asking of the universe with respect to our lives. If we send out negative, judgmental vibes then that is exactly what will befall us in one form or another.

We need to develop positive and empowering thoughts, questions, and ways to communicate that keep us open to the infinite possibility that exists in each moment. We need to consciously utilize this way of communicating to show our unconscious that it is safe to communicate in this way and experience the results that will come to us if we continue the Four C Process.

It is even in our best interest to rethink 'joking' remarks about others and ourselves. Thoughts and spoken words carry weight to them. There is an energy, a vibe, within these. Do we jokingly put ourselves down or put others down? How will this type of 'playfully negative' energy impact lives? What about just communicating negatively in general? How will this impact our lives in the present and what we believe we can be in the future? Are we hopeful in our communication? Are we open-minded? How's your communication?

2.8 Commitment

If this word hasn't been evident up to this point in the book it is an absolute necessity. If we aren't committed to changing or learning or growing or receiving a different result then how can we expect a different one. We better reconsider our resolve and commitment to accomplish what we say we want to.

If we want change and we want to stay committed we need to hold ourselves or we need to have someone else (at least in the beginning) hold us accountable. How many people have said they want to change but aren't really fully invested in making the commitment. Talking about making the commitment can make us feel like we're actually going to do something but it's usually the exact opposite; that we're just putting it off. We're just creating a false future hope.

I think we need to be a little wary of how we use the word commitment. If we are actually following through and are committed that's fantastic! But if we're talking about committing, feeling good, and then taking no action we better be careful. How many people have said, *I'll quit smoking tomorrow, I'll start going to the gym tomorrow, (maybe the best one) I'll start my diet tomorrow (so I'll eat whatever I want and as much as I want right now!).*

Commitment isn't something that you do in the future it's a decision you make and an action you take in the present.

Stop using it as a feel good word in the moment when you actually have no intention to commit to anything that would get you unstuck in the present. Commitment implies action to some end *right now*. As I said before, you're not committed to it if you're going to do it tomorrow because tomorrow never comes.

2.9 Clarity

In order to be successful in a certain area in your life it's a good idea to get clear on what you would like to accomplish and keep those front-of-mind always. If you don't have clarity on what you want, what you're good at, who you want to be, etc. then *how* are you going to *be it, have it,* or *do it*? Your unconscious mind is incredibly good at keeping things unclear and keeping you away from clarity.

To me clarity implies that you have some kind of vision. It would be as if the clouds have parted and in the distance you can see your end goal clearly and you can see in front of you the path laid out that is going to take you there all that's left to do is take action and walk the path.

To be able to get clear on your path forward and your goals in life the best place to start is with the Four C Process. Start by asking empowering questions. What are the things that you want to do? You can start with smaller questions and ideas. For example, questions related to eating healthier, getting more physical activity, joining a book club, painting, education, networking, or whatever it is you want to work on. You can also start by asking larger questions to. Remember you don't have to know *how* everything is going to look or feel but over time things should become more clear as you begin breaking down the unconscious mind and breaking down the habits that have kept you from achieving your full potential for so long.

The reason why clarity is so important to develop over time is that if you're not clear on what you want then how are you supposed to receive it? It is absolutely essential that we continue to fine tune what things are going to look, feel, taste, sound, and smell like. Get *that* specific!

Here's an example, Monday morning you decide that you really want to checkout the new restaurant down the street from work. You have no idea when it's going to happen but you are sure you are going to make it happen. You want to go with someone so what do you do? You start asking people and no matter how many people say they can't you keep asking and finally you find someone to go with and then what do you do? You set the day and the time. Now it's going to happen just like you planned it!

This is the way we should be with the goals that we want to achieve in our life. We can have an end goal in mind then we have to start fine-tuning the plan and making small steps and plans within the larger vision so that we know we're on tracking towards achieving it.

Write down some goals and when you do listen for the little unconscious mind's voice that's going to undoubtedly come out and try and turn you off of those big audacious goals that you have. Do *not* be deterred. Get curious about this little voice and get your conscious mind to ask empowering and enlightening questions so that it can develop strength over your unconscious mind. Continue to write down your goals daily. Get into the habit so that you're thinking about it, writing it, saying it, and hearing it. You could even post your goals in different places around your car, home, or office, etc. to be constantly reminded of what it is you are working toward and are going to stop at nothing to achieve it.

Visualization is another important tool that I think of when I think of getting clear on your goals. You want to create a detailed picture in your mind of what you want to achieve. If you listen to people talk about how they accomplished whatever they did sometimes they refer to the fact that they visualized the result, their success, or whatever it was, over, and over, and over again. Visualization is a very powerful tool to assist you in achieving what you want to in your life.

2.10 Congruence

Ah, congruence, the art of *practicing what you preach*. This means speaking, acting, living, and being in alignment with your purpose and your ultimate goal.

Here's an excuse for not living in alignment; *but I'm only human*. Sure we're human. Our actions tell us what's most important to us. One of my favourite actions that is completely out of alignment and congruence is *yelling, 'STOP YELLING SO MUCH! QUIET DOWN!* Now, if you can't see this statement is completely out of whack, then read this book a few more times. You are essentially, in case it's not clear, *yelling to stop yelling*. You might as well be saying two wrongs make a right.

Living in congruence with your purpose on a daily and moment-to-moment basis is something to strive toward. It's maintaining a hopeful optimism to have this as our ultimate goal. Our conscious selves are best served when our vision, actions, and words are in alignment with our individual gifts. This includes the purpose we were given to be on this planet and our striving every day to ensure others are better off for us having graced this earth.

My saying is *Strive To Optimize*. If we keep this in mind with everything we do we will be on the right track. We should always be working towards bettering ourselves, fine tuning and re-clarifying our vision, acting and speaking from our highest conscious self, and rectifying the discord and disconnect between our unconscious and conscious selves.

    We must recognize that we are already perfect in the way we were created. The ultimate achievement in life is realigning ourselves so that we may share our best self with the world.

2.11 Celebrate

Think about it. Life should really be a celebration! It should be fun! It should be energizing! It should be purposeful! It should be filled with laughs! It should be filled with friends! It should be filled with love!

When you're curious about something and you cultivate it and become confident in and then collaborate with others don't you feel *GREAT!* You feel amazing to be so competent in an area and be at the point where you can share and continue to develop your interests and the love of the area that you're so curious about!

That's why I love the quote I shared at the beginning of the book. In the quote, your can replace curiosity with *love, having fun, happiness, joy, positivity, success, living with purpose*. Try it! Would you ever get tired of being successful, of loving and being loved, of having fun, of being happy, of feeling joy, of feeling and expressing positivity, of living with purpose? *Would you seriously ever, and I mean EVER, get sick of ANY of those things? Wouldn't we all LOVE to have that?* Our conscious mind is like *yes, yes, yes, yes, YES! Keep it coming please!* Our unconscious mind is suspicious, is uncertain, is fearful, and is scared. The unconscious mind will say, *yaaaaa but (AND THERE'S THE INFAMOUS BUT) those things can't, don't, won't, and are impossible to last forever.* And the conscious mind, for some of us, *ACTUALLY BELIEVE THIS SH!T! ARE YOU SERIOUS?* I don't know about you but aren't you tired of listening to and believing that unconscious mind? Ask your conscious mind and listen to it for the split second before the unconscious mind steps in, takes over, and throws a million doubts into your mind in less than five seconds!

The Four C Process will help quiet the unconscious mind because we're focusing on small, manageable steps, that focus on things that we're already good at and the unconscious mind is familiar with and it won't get triggered. Then we keep pushing the boundaries of the limits of the unconscious mind and eventually the unconscious mind actually jumps on board with the conscious mind and all of the things that you're accomplishing and all the positivity, happiness, success, and love you're experiencing!

The journey of life should be celebrated and if we did this we would be more proud of ourselves and more often. Remember, the unconscious mind is focused on *lack* and the conscious mind's focus is *possibility*, which begins with curiosity and is *endless*! We're just so unaccustomed to listening to the conscious mind that its voice is so quiet and limited in our lives. We need to practice hearing it and celebrate the journey toward achieving and being everything we want to in our lives.

2.12 Creativity

The Four C process *will* start the creative juices going. Curiosity opens our conscious minds up to possibility and this will stimulate our creativity because we open ourselves up to the world of ideas. Creativity is so important because it allows us to adapt and be one with time and space.

We can apply creativity to our businesses, our personal lives, our relationships, our interests; absolutely *anything*. Creativity allows us to think about endless possibilities.

Here's my analogy of creativity; *The Blank Canvas*. Someone hands you a canvas. The look in their eyes says to you that it's your job to create something. Something for yourself. You are in room with anything you could possibly need to create something with your canvas. It is up to you to decide what and how to use the resources you have. You think to yourself, *but wait I am no artist. I have had no experience in creating anything that is representative of art. Why have I been given this opportunity?* The person that has handed you the canvas looks back at you. You feel them saying that you do not need any experience to create something. You, not being one to reject a gift, accept the canvas. You understand that the task at hand is now to create something upon this canvas. You free your mind, let it go and begin searching curiously around to find the materials that are going to make this canvas into something that is perfect for yourself.

This small analogy is representative of a person's life. Life is your canvas. Life is your gift. The type of canvas, or life, that we're given is a matter of circumstance. We don't necessarily get to choose where the *canvas* begins its journey. However, from these initial circumstances it does become our choice of how to act. Action is a matter of choice; just as perception is. If we see ourselves simply *as the canvas* how will we ever know what to make? We'll believe that we have nothing to offer because we are simply a blank canvas.

But what if we were both the canvas *and* the artist? What then? If we were both the canvas and the artist and had unlimited resources from which to create a masterful piece what would we do then? People become overwhelmed with life because they feel like they're just a canvas. What purpose does a blank canvas serve? The beauty of life is that we are *both* the canvas *and* the artist and that the possibilities with what *we can create* are infinite. Infinite possibility.

People's creativity has not been blocked in the areas of their life where they succeeded in the Four C Process. But the areas where people don't believe in their abilities to create something for themselves have a creative block. If we think of a child's creativity; theirs is endless. They are curious and they create. They create with gestures, sounds, noises, movements, stories, and games. They know how to visualize and the people who become most successful are those that never lose their ability to visualize and learn how to turn them into actualizations and materializations.

Creativity has no boundaries. Truly it does not. It is infinite.

What does our current canvas look like? What have we used our imagination for? This is an important question, one that people may disagree with but nonetheless it is the truth. Our life, right now, is what we've imagined it to be. Our visualizations, whether conscious or not, have become actualized. The great thing about creativity is that, as I have said, it has no end and no beginning. We can 'begin' to pay more attention to what our visualizations are and turn them into the actualizations and materializations that we want.

How to get there? There must be change. Our lives are filled with patterns; patterns of repeated behaviours, feelings, thoughts, and moments. We reinforce these patterns through our unconscious mind on an ongoing basis; a daily basis. These patterned repetitions have taken us on a journey through life to where we are today. Sometimes we become clouded by the emotion of our circumstances. Through our emotions we reinforce our unconscious pattern loops.

If we are not happy with where we've ended up where is the last place we look but the first place we should? Ourselves.

Instead of looking at ourselves we look for reasons and for people who are the cause of our circumstances. Our unconscious mind is an expert at looking outside of itself to validate how it is feeling and to reinforce its categorizations, definitions, and labels about life and circumstances. Our unconscious mind has trained us to remain unconscious and continually look outside of ourselves for answers that can only be resolved within.

We've long forgotten the curiosity of childhood. We've forgotten our imagination. We've forgotten how to create. We've forgotten the times we could just invent, on the spot, anything we wanted to that would become part of the game we were playing in our mind. We've forgotten how powerful we *are*.

We fantasize about stopping time and holding onto it or of going back in time and becoming young again. We believe that's the only way to achieve what we're missing. We believe, that if we could only be transported to a time that *isn't here and now*, we'd find and have what we were looking for. What we're looking for we already have. It's the boundless creativity within us all. Children don't need to wait for the right time to be creative. They will create any time, any where, any place. We're trained to mature, grow up, smarten up, etc. and through this we lose the one thing we will always long for: our connection with our own innate creative spirit. However, we haven't just lost sight of our creative spirit, we've lost our belief in our ability to create our own reality.

So stop. Take a look at your canvas (your life), how does it look? What do you want to add to it? Artistic creations take time but a true artist is never deterred by time. They imagine, they visualize and they will stop at nothing to actualize their vision and dreams.

Be open, be curious, and above all, visualize what you want to actualize and materialize.

2.13 Courage

The journey within is not for the faint of heart. It can feel like admitting you're wrong to someone you strongly dislike except the person you strongly dislike in this case is yourself, specifically your unconscious mind. The journey within does require courage to face yourself and to own up to your own B.S. that has kept you stuck for however long you've been alive. Your unconscious mind is like that ride at the theme park that spins around extremely fast and you're standing up and it pushes your entire body against the wall and to move even your foot is a struggle. That's the way facing your mind can be. It can feel like even taking one step off course is the biggest struggle and you can't believe the resistance you're facing.

You have curiosity, you have courage, and you can *definitely do this!*

2.14 Camaraderie

This could possibly be the most important thing in this book. *Use your support network!* I cannot stress this enough. Going down the path toward confronting your unconscious mind can be a very dark path. If you don't have support around you, of people or mentors who are extremely supportive and understanding or who have been there before themselves, you might get into trouble. Facing your unconscious mind can be real hell on earth. You better be fully committed to finding what you seek.

I believe you can make the changes you need to or want to. Make sure you have someone there who feels the same way. There is *always hope.*

2.15 Choice

What you accomplish in your life is up to you. You *do* have the ultimate say in what that is. I did an interesting calculation recently that put TV in perspective in a way that I hadn't thought about it before. Recently I cut TV out of my life, which was definitely something I had wanted to do but had never really made the commitment. So I did the math and if someone watches 2 hours of TV per day for 365 days a year that's 730 hours of TV in one year. Now divide 730 hours by 24 hours in a day and you get almost 30 and a half days (30.42). This means that if you watch 2 hours of TV each day for 1 year you will have watched the equivalent of 30.42 *straight days of TV with no breaks*. Thinking of it in this way is really astounding to me! If you kept watching TV at that rate then in 12 years you will have watched the equivalent of *1 full year of TV non-stop!*

Now there are many people whose television watching matches or exceeds 2 hours/day. Think about the time investment you're making with your life! Isn't that an incredible way to think about the time you spend watching TV? I thought it was fascinating! Think about what you could accomplish in one year if instead of dedicating just over 30 days of your precious time to TV you actually dedicated it to something you are absolutely passionate about. What would your life look like if you made that simple choice? I'll leave the rest up to you.

The Overarching C

Change

When it hasn't been stated it's been implied throughout this book. Overarching all of these words, examples, and analogies is change. Just as someone can never step into the same river twice, so too with our lives. Each moment is new and precious. Life is synonymous with change. This one word summarizes life in an objective way and signifies everything that humans attempt to come to grips with in their world.

We have the ability to foster, nurture, and develop change in our lives or we can try and turn it off but will forever fail at stopping change. Our unconscious mind is *not* a fan of change. Our unconscious mind would be happy if our basic needs were met and nothing of ourselves was ever challenged. Our conscious mind knows and believes in the possibility that comes with change and sees it as an exciting opportunity. Change opens our eyes, fills us with energy and desire to complete anything and everything that is most important to us.

In our personal lives and in our businesses we have to be able to adapt to the changes that are always happening in technology, science, our community, our state, other people, our clients, our consumers, our relationships, etc. The unconscious mind has difficulty with these and with all of change. The conscious mind sees all of these as opportunities to learn, grow, develop, explore, and experience. This is why tuning into our conscious mind is so important. The conscious mind will say things like: *You should really go and talk to them. You should really share this idea with the team. You should go for a walk right now.* It probably takes a second for the unconscious mind to jump all over these ideas and snuff them out and deny us of the opportunities present within these and countless other moments.

Nothing in the world is static. Even if we look at physical structures that look static, if we were able to look at them through a lens that allowed us to see their molecular structure we would see the movement, the vibration, and the energy that exists at this level. Everything in this world is dynamic and in constant motion. The world is a marvel just as each one of us are and we need to give a voice to and take action for our conscious mind that wants to express, create, discover, learn, grow, and connect.

Even if things are moving back and forth between 2 points, they're still moving. They are never static. Going back to that notion that life is like a river. You may try sticking your hand into the river and try to grasp a handful of water but you will never be successful. Just as in life, we unconsciously try to hold onto a moment and we become unconsciously linked to this moment (in our past), we will never be able to actually hold that moment.

Just as a moment comes, it goes.

I just want to go a little more in depth with the idea of trying to 'grasp water'. The fact that water cannot be grasped by a human's hand (don't believe me? Try grabbing a fist full of water, you will always come up empty-handed) has not deterred humans from finding alternative means to grasp or contain water.

For humans, how would we exist if we didn't have language with which to communicate our feelings, thoughts, ideas, hopes, etc. Language was become absolutely essential for us in order to communicate with others. Life and water in the following analogy are synonymous to one another.

The Water Analogy. Let's imagine we have buckets in millions of different shapes and sizes with which we can 'hold water'. We take all of the buckets and fill them with water from the river. By doing this we can define the water but it is all based on the container that it fills. Without the bucket how do we explain, define, and understand the water? Who created the buckets? Humans did. Therefore, is our experience of water based on its infiniteness or on the finiteness of the shape it has taken from being scooped up in the bucket? If we lined up hundreds of thousands of buckets each of different shapes and sizes, all filled with water would our understanding of the water contained in each of the buckets be based on water itself or of the buckets that it filled?

As humans we look at these buckets and we describe *the water* when really we can only describe the water that way because of the bucket it is in. So it's the bucket that forms our perception of the water but *we believe* and *communicate* to each other the description of the water and disregard the fact that we can only describe it that way because of the container it is in.

Now let's bring the analogy back to our lives and how it relates. Water and life are analogous to one another in the same way that the buckets and our language (social constructs) are analogous to one another. So what does this mean? So the definitions and labels of our unconscious mind's filing cabinet system are our buckets and as we go through life we fill up these 'buckets' with life. Therefore, we don't see life as it is; in it's infiniteness and that it is really beyond all social constructs, labels, definitions, and language. We view life through which 'buckets' we place life in and this is completely occurring in our unconscious mind.

Do our labels, definitions, and social constructs actually exist outside of ourselves? Do they exist outside of our unconscious mind? Most will say yes. We don't need to look to far to know that if we view life in a certain way we know of someone else who thinks, feels, or expresses themselves in a similar manner. Just because you find someone else who thinks, feels, or expresses like you does that mean it should justify your point of view? That's what we always do though. Our unconscious mind runs through its loops and then it likes to reaffirm how it's feeling. So we take life, throw it into a bucket that we have shaped and then look for someone else who's made the same kind of bucket with which to contain life because our unconscious mind wants to continually strengthen its beliefs and views of the world.

This is why it's so difficult to raise our level of consciousness. Our unconscious mind is an expert at strengthening itself and it comes so naturally to us. Human beings have practiced strengthening their unconscious minds for centuries.

Our views, beliefs, expectations, labels, and definitions are literally the buckets with which we shape life. If we view ourselves as *stupid* we take our life, our actions, our interactions and we literally place our life in the *stupid bucket* that we have. So the only reason we're experiencing life as a 'stupid' person is because we have a 'stupid bucket' in our mind and that's what our life fills. What a great illusion! This concept of reality *only* exists in the bucket that is in our mind and literally does not exist anywhere else.

What if there is a child who's seen as smart? Therefore, so much of what they do fills the 'smart bucket' in other people's minds. Eventually the child may also feel that they are smart and will have their own 'smart bucket' in their mind that their life continually fills. What a great bucket to have in your mind! Who wouldn't want to have that kind of label and be living up to that?

What happens with language, definitions, social constructs, and these 'buckets' is that they can literally create, for us, resistance to change. If we are resisting change we are resisting possibility. If we resist change then our possibilities are limited because of the buckets we place our life into. If we place our lives into buckets that limit our potential will we find or experience hope that we can change our lives anytime we want?

Are we the ones who created language? No. But we are the ones who've interpreted language and impressed it upon our lives. We've done this unconsciously, never knowing the implications of allowing certain words, phrases, and beliefs to become apart of our unconscious mind's filing cabinet system. We attach our life's meaning and purpose to these 'buckets', categories, and social constructs. However, life, in reality, exists entirely outside of these 'buckets', categories, and social constructs.

The most important question is WHY have these 'buckets', categories, and social constructs been created in the first place? Humans want to be able to communicate with each other so we have language, which includes labels, in order to communicate our understanding to another person.

Language attempts to define our experience and, in a way, we're attempting to exert our control over the world. We do that with our 'buckets', categories, and social constructs and everything that makes up our societies, cities, countries, and world attempts to grasp that water from the river of change that will continually and eternally flow. We try to own that piece of water. We try to control that piece of water. We try and manipulate that piece of water to suit our own needs. Social constructs exist because we want to know who people are and we think that they can be contained within a label whose definition has a generalized notion that more than likely does grasp some of that person but can a person be contained within a label in their entirety? Can water's true essence be contained within a bucket? A person and water are one and the same and their essence and nature can never truly be contained within a category or bucket because language is finite and how can something finite grasp something that is infinite.

In addition, whether water is contained within a bucket or a person within a label it implies that the object being contained is fixed, idle, and unchanging. This is an illusion that *only exists* within the bucket and within the label. Outside of such constructs the rules that qualify or quantify the bucket or label do not exist. If we become fixated on idleness we can liken ourselves to those who didn't believe the Earth orbited around the sun. It is easy to see the unconscious minds at work in the past and their unaccepting behaviour toward brilliant and forward thinking people. Let us not fall into that trap and believe that we ourselves are somehow hopeless people unable to change ourselves to whatever it is that we would like to see ourselves become in this world.

Important Non-C Words For Success

1. Gratitude

There can't be enough said about gratitude. Gratitude is your friend. Gratitude is your ally. Gratitude is a practice. There are so many things in life that we simply take for granted. We are unappreciative. We are ungrateful. We overlook things. They're not even in our circle of awareness. Too much of our lives are lived in unconsciousness.

Too much of our time and attention can be spent on negative thoughts, feelings, imagery, experiences, worries about what is, what isn't and what could have been. There are countless ways that our minds are taken away from a state of gratitude. Again, this is all at the unconscious level because we're not even aware of the loops that are running in the back of our minds.

Here's my analogy for what we do in our lives. I'll call this the *I Spy Analogy*.

Do you remember playing the *I spy* game growing up? Maybe I've dated myself, I'm not sure if people are playing that anymore. I mean there are probably more vehicles with built-in DVD players and almost everyone has a Tablet or other hand held device so that they can occupy their time with mindlessness. But back to the game. This is how the game is played. One person says, *I spy with my little eye something that is* _____ (and you can insert anything there). Let's say the person says, *something that is red*. Now, everyone else has to look around in the car and find that one red item that the person saw. Whoever finds the red item then gets to look for something and says what they spy and everyone else guesses, and so on.

Okay, so what's the point? The point is that I don't think we've ever stopped playing the game and even people who have never played this game play it currently in their lives. How? Well, the way that we've come to play the game is that we don't play it with shapes or colours, we play it with *feelings* and *events*.

During our daily lives we look for things that fulfill our unconscious thought patterns for the way we *feel*. And too much of our attention can, at times, get caught up on *negative* feelings. We don't need to look very far for this. The imagery and general tone of 99% of media coverage is negative. It's filled with killings, stabbings, robberies, accidents, traffic jams, weather (which *really* upsets people for some reason), natural disasters, other tragedies, etc. When we feel sad, what are we going to do? We don't necessarily jump to looking for something that's going to be uplifting. For example, if we wake up and we're unhappy for whatever reason we'll say, *I'm tired, I'm depressed, I can't believe the weather is so terrible today, I don't want to go to work today, etc.* When we feel a certain way we *look for* or *think about* (past, present, or future events) things that are going to *reaffirm* the way that we feel!

So instead of just waking up and not feeling very happy and try to shake it off we *choose* and *want* to remain in the state we're in and say *I spy with my little eye something that is <u>depressing</u> or* _annoying_ or _frustrating_ or whatever we can think of. Then we continue to move through our day but it's never certain what mood we're going to be in because we _don't feel we have the power to change anything._ We can get living too reactively sometimes and not more proactively, which would give us an opportunity to change our mental state and the way we feel.

If we want to change the way we feel it doesn't necessarily change instantaneously unless we practice. We need to practice things that are going to allow us to be more conscious, energetic, passionate, loving, grateful, and caring. An absolutely fantastic idea is starting a gratitude journal. Each night (or whenever you want to) pull out your journal that's already beside your bed with a pen in it and write a few things that you're thankful for. Get your mind thinking about all of the things that you're thankful for. If you do this consistently it will actually change the way your mind is wired because how often do we review our day and list all of the fantastic things that happened, or that we did, or just little things that we appreciate so much. This will help to focus our minds and attention on positive things. When we've developed this habit then we'll be going through our day and saying to ourselves _oh I better remember this so that I can write it in my journal tonight_. We'll be consciously looking for reasons and things to be thankful for. This is an excellent way to rewire and refocus our brains and it's such a simple task.

In addition, it's even something you could share with your partner at night too so that each of you could know about other positive things that happened in each other's day.

2. Love

Personally speaking, I'm not sure if I can really separate love and gratitude because I believe each exists in the other. I want to mention love though because it is such an important word. It is so much more than a word that I don't think it can even be captured by the word's simplicity. It means so much more than that.

For me love is seeing beyond the person and the physical reality and experiencing their spirit. It is having a deep understanding of the other person, their values and their strengths. It is looking at a person beyond the realm of judgment and discernment through which our unconscious mind views the world.

To me, love cannot actually be given and it can definitely never be taken away. Love *is* all of existence. I think of this law from physics often; *energy cannot be created or destroyed*. To me this is the love; this is the spirit that exists in everyone and everything. We are a part of it and forever connected. In it there exists the world of infinite possibility and endless strength. To me life is a journey through which we strive to raise our level of consciousness and awareness and to recognize our connection to love, to spirit, to energy, and to each other; we are all really *one*.

3. Accountability/Responsibility

The word *responsibility* has gotten a bad rap for some reason, and come to be mistakenly thought of as a 'chore'. Perhaps it's the way we were taught as children that this thing and that thing were our responsibilities. Because they weren't our own ideas, in our minds these tasks were perceived as chores, so as a result, we continue view responsibilities as chores. I'm sure there are some good and curious questions that could be thought of to further our understanding of the relationship between responsibilities and chores.

Generally, the things we love to do are our responsibilities and we complete these tasks. For the things that we dislike to do we run from our responsibilities. However, what happens sometimes is that because we aren't truly grateful for something or appreciative of it we start taking it for granted and when we do this, what was once a joyous responsibility becomes a *burden that we must bear*. If we are able to bring ourselves back to a place of gratitude, we would better, and more joyously and energetically, complete our responsibilities.

Not everyone sees their physical, mental, emotional, and spiritual aspects of themselves as responsibilities. We may be good in some areas but we may also be lacking in other areas. I like to think that for the areas that we neglect we've fallen out of a place of gratitude. We unconsciously view that to maintain and be responsible to ourselves and that aspect of our self is a complete burden and we have no energy or intention of changing it. We are reluctant *and* we neglect it. In addition, some of us will only move toward making a change in our life if tragedy strikes. Take for example, our physical health, someone *may* (and it's still *only* a maybe) look to become more responsible for their physical health if they have a heart attack. But if you leave it to that point you may not get the opportunity to do so.

We need to start taking a proactive approach to our physical, mental, emotional, and spiritual bodies. We *must* practice specific routines that will keep each of these aspects aligned within ourselves. We must not wait until tragedy strikes. But change will only come from a place of gratitude, respect, and curiosity. If we learn to be thankful for each of these aspects we will become curious as to how we can achieve full health in all areas within ourselves. This is representative of true love toward oneself and most certainly, self-love is an area in which we could all use more practice.

The hope would be to become more responsible for our life. This would lead to *actually taking ownership of our life!* Think about that! We don't even feel confident that we are responsible for our physical, mental, emotional, and spiritual self. We are! We *can* take back our lives and create a space, within ourselves, that we are *proud* to call home!

4. Action

Where would we be without action? In order to experience love and gratitude and alignment within ourselves we *must* take action. Our life's work cannot be achieved passively. So many people are *waiting*. We're *waiting for the right time, the right person, the right circumstance, the right conditions, the right feeling, the right thought*. We wait and wait and wait and wait but life continues to pass us by and nobody ever comes to save us from what has become our miserable existence and then we cry out, *why me?! Why haven't I been saved?! Why hasn't my life changed?! Why doesn't it get any better?! Why am I still stuck here?! Why do I still feel this way?! WHY, WHY, WHY, WHY, WHY?!*

Let me save you the suspense. Nobody is coming. Nobody is coming to save you from the way you're feeling in this moment. *We* need to take ownership. *We* need to take responsibility for our circumstances, feelings, thoughts, and life. *We* need to *take action* to change our life so that it is reflective of something we are incredibly proud of!

5. Patience

In the age where immediacy is an implicit expectation, the value of patience cannot be overstated. Guess what? We *have* time. We have it! Guess what? Things *take time.* It will take time to accomplish things in your life but avoiding action will not get you closer to living the life of your dreams. In addition, disempowering questions don't help us with achieving anything. For example, *how am I going to find the time? How am I going to find balance? How am I going to find the capital? How am I going to find the resources? How am I going to lose weight? How am I going to be happy?* These questions are the same as *what if* questions. What if this, what if that, etc. They're completely disempowering. We need to be patient with receiving answers literally *from the Universe* by asking empowering questions that keep us open to all possibility.

The funny thing about patience is that it will take practice to become more patient. We have to learn to be able to wait for answers, wait for our actions to bear the fruit that we want. As Auguste Rodin said, *patience is also a form of action.*

6. Resources

Resources are all around you. If you want to start working out look for people within your network that work out or are physically active. If you don't have people in your network who are physically active then guess what? You have to expand your network. You have to step outside of your comfort zone. You have to step outside of the comfort zone of the unconscious mind's boundaries that it has set for you and upon you. Resources are all around us if we're looking for them. It's just like when you buy a new car that you rarely see on the road but once you buy it all of a sudden you see that car every single place that you go because that is what you're focusing on.

If there's a certain job that you want are there people in your network that you know who have that job? If there aren't then you need to start expanding your network and seeking out the people who have those jobs, so that you can learn more about them.

If you run a business and your comfort zone is your current specific client base, but you would like to grow your business and attract new clients, guess what? It's time to step outside of your comfort zone, expand your network, and look for resources that are going to help you achieve your goals.

Phase Three: Final Thoughts, Reflections & Analogies

Your Core

Everyone has certain strengths, abilities, skills, knowledge, experiences that make them unique and are a part of who they are. A great tragedy in life is that we don't share these often enough with other people. Even worse is that we don't believe these qualities that we have are of any value to ourselves and others?

These passions, interests, strengths, abilities, skills, etc. are the core of who you are and it's about time you started believing in them and sharing them with others. The Four C Process will not only help you to start paying more attention to the areas you've been avoiding, they will also direct you to the areas that will help you reach a level of satisfaction you didn't believe you could obtain before.

We need to think of ourselves in terms of these uplifting and empowering skills. If we're going to place any labels on ourselves they should fall into categories like, empowering, inspiring, motivating, engaging, loving, and uplifting. The only labels we should use to describe ourselves are ones like: confident, energetic, passionate, successful, loving, caring, talented, athletic, insightful, creative, engaged, artistic, charismatic, outgoing, etc. We should focus on words like these especially when we are trying to make changes in our life. We're used to using words that have negative associations and we place them upon ourselves on a daily basis. We need to become more aware of them and cut them out entirely (which would be ideal), especially when we're just starting out on the path to change.

These positive characteristics that each of us possess truly represent the core of who we are; the centre of our being. They are the most important aspects of who we are and what we can contribute to the world and it's about time we started living from this *core* within ourselves.

Rethinking Leadership

When most people think about leadership they think about others. They think about business owners, managers, supervisors, CEOs, coaches, and how they lead others and lead us. In our journeys through life, leadership is an excellent way to approach life for *ourselves*. We need to view our life as something that *we are leading*. It seems as though there is a lot of emphasis on finding solutions to life's problems outside of ourselves because we don't believe, strongly enough, the power we have to effect change in our own life. Our unconscious mind is afraid of what the conscious mind is fully capable of achieving.

More recently in human history, there has been a natural shift and focus toward ourselves in order to find the solutions to what ails us. Activities and practices such as yoga, meditation, living more healthfully and diets, and physical activity have become more focused on as avenues to heal our lives. As such, reflecting on the idea of leadership and how it applies to our lives is an excellent way to learn more about ourselves as we continue on in our journey through life.

There is no single 'key' to life; to finding success, happiness, health, love, purpose, and so forth. People have to find their own way. Said another way, there is no prescription to find and have everything that we need and want.

Let's reflect on an analogy to shed light on the idea of

leadership and how it applies to each of our lives. *The Leadership Analogy*. Sarah wants to lose some weight and get stronger. Sarah's never worked out before and has no idea what she's doing in a gym and therefore enlists the expertise, guidance, and assistance of a personal trainer, Ted. Ted's been a personal trainer for over 20 years and is great at his job. He'll take the time to assess Sarah's current physical condition through some physical testing and get an idea about her background and past and present health conditions. Ted completes his assessment, which includes finding out about Sarah's goals related to their work together. Sarah is keen to get started and transform her life and Ted develops a plan that will slowly challenge her and start her on the path toward reaching her goals that she and Ted have outlined together. Ted will be by her side at the gym, motivating and encouraging her through their sessions. Ted's area of expertise is in physical conditioning but he likes to make sure that his clients enlist the help and support of others as well and helps Sarah get connected with other gym members and other service providers in the community to explore areas such as nutrition and diet, yoga, etc. to help supplement the work that she and Ted will be doing together.

Sarah makes progress over the coming weeks and months although not without challenges. Ted continually adapts his plan with Sarah to her ever-changing needs and progress. In the work that Ted does he always ensures his professionalism, integrity and holds himself accountable to high standards, to his client's success, and to his organization's standards as well. Ted leads by example within the gym and within the community and ensures he's always practicing what he preaches. He supports his clients and continually reassesses and reflects on their level of satisfaction, their goals, and their progress. Both Ted and Sarah follow through with their commitments and responsibilities to themselves and each other. They both take action to achieve what they have set out to.

How does this analogy relate to leadership? Both individuals are exhibiting leadership characteristics. Let's look at some of the characteristics that they both exhibit: commitment, taking responsibility, ownership, follow through, action, setting goals, and having a plan, to name a few. What happens if the trainer-trainee relationship between Ted and Sarah ends (for whatever reason)? Sarah may or may not seek another personal trainer. Let's assume she's been working with Ted for a couple of years and she's met all of the goals she had in mind. If she no longer works with Ted she could either decide to find a new personal trainer or she, having learned all that she wanted to or mastered a wide variety of exercises that are important to her goals, could decide to be her own leader and motivator to maintain her physical health. Moving forward, Sarah may decide to do some research on the internet to find new physical activity related exercises, she may speak with friends, family, other gym members, she may join a group fitness class, or she may eventually enlist the services of another personal trainer.

What are some qualities that Sarah is exhibiting now? They

would be similar to when she first began to seek out assistance with achieving her physical health goals. She would be motivated, ready to take action, curious, driven to improve, looking to cultivate or develop her knowledge, skills, and physical health, increase her confidence as she continues to learn and grow, and collaborate with others, sharing both her experiences and knowledge.

So what has transpired? Sarah has become an expert to the extent that it is important for her in her life. Because, remember, we are only talking about one aspect of her life. In other words, and the point that I want to drive home, she is, even before the analogy began being described, in the past, present, and future, a leader for herself in this aspect of her life. She may have enlisted the service of Ted to lead her in a direction of her life but she is still the leader of her own life and is going after what she wants to do and accomplish for herself. Ted was just there to help her along the journey and path that she chose for her life.

Sarah is the leader in and for her life. Ted is not the leader of her life. Ted is just a guiding influence during a certain stage in Sarah's life. The leaders, coaches, managers, bosses, parents, and so forth are just people of influence in the paths of our life. Some will have lengthy relationships with us. Some will continue to affect us as we move forward because of the lasting impact they had on us and our personalities, whereas some will enter and leave our lives more quickly. Everyone in our lives, for better or for worse, serves a purpose for us along the journey of our lives.

As the leader of our life we are BOTH the trainer and trainee.

But the fact is, we're not always going to have a 'Ted' around. Sure, having a 'Ted' would definitely be nice but there are going to be times when we're going to have to do things on our own. We're going to have to take on Ted's characteristics and be that motivator, that inspiration, that support, that caring person, that organized person, that committed person. We're going to have to do those things for *ourselves*. That means when you want to be that unmotivated, lazy *trainee*, your *'trainer self'* needs to wake up and whip you back into shape so you can stay focused on your goals.

From each situation and person there is a reminder, a lesson to be learned. There are times when all we see is what we always see as we peer through our subjective and unconscious lens at the world around us. There are other times when a person, experience, or thought or idea will penetrate that subjective lenses and connect with an objective reality and allow us to see, think, hear, touch, or feel connected to a deeper reality that connects us all. So much attention and focus is on ourselves and our subjective reality but not in a way where we pay attention to the objective reality we are all equally a part of.

We do have control over our responses and receptiveness to the world around us. A business owner has control over their business, not the market, not it's customers, just their business. Is a business owner going to blame consumer behaviour or its competition for losing market share? If the business owner just sits back and blames, which they're more than welcome to do because it is their choice, they will certainly not be in business very long. The business owner needs foresight, needs to learn about and understand its consumers, its competitors, its market enough so that the business owner can incorporate these things into their vision for their business and their business's future.

The same can be said for each individual person. We, as individuals, don't necessarily have control over other people, our relationships, our employment, our genetics, our community, our society, our country, our world. However, we do have control of how we respond to everything around us including our environment, our circumstances, our situations, and the people within it. If something isn't happening in our lives the way that we want it to then what are we doing to change it? Are we waiting for a leader or mentor, or person to come save us from our situation and provide us with everything good in our lives? We need to hold ourselves accountable for our own life's choices. We need to rethink leadership in that it's not something others do to and for us but that we must do for ourselves. We must lead ourselves toward the future we envision for our lives.

The Movie Analogy

You play the leading role in the movie of your life. Imagine you, the director and producers are the primary Cs. Together you are all of primary importance in setting the stage for the movie of your life. The secondary Cs are equally important and they represent the supporting cast and crew in the movie of your life. In the movie of your life is everything and everyone coming together to produce a movie that you would want to play the lead role in? Is it a movie that would stimulate energy, passion, connection, emotion, etc. within you if you were in the audience?

Here's *The Movie Analogy*. There's a movie in the works that everyone is talking about. The movie is bringing together the best cast and crew to have ever been in the same movie. The best director, producers, editors, costume designers, music crew, etc. and the absolute best actors and actresses. What would make them the best in their craft? They would have practiced for years and they would have developed processes that help them prepare for the roles that they play within the movie.

This movie has an unlimited budget and resources and it's expected to be the best movie ever made. The entire cast and crew that has come together to create this film is unprecedented. Every movie fan and movie buff can't wait to see the result. Except I've left out one piece. They *don't* have a *script*. How could they have overlooked this most obvious piece?

Our lives are no different. Our unique qualities, attributes, skills, abilities, strengths, and gifts have come together in an unprecedented way. At no point in the history of our planet has someone been formed with your uniqueness. The audience of the world is waiting and watching to see what incredible life you're going to create. Don't forget the most important piece. Don't forget *your script!* You are here to not only write out your script but to live it out.

The actors and actresses that have mastered their craft relate to us too. Just as they have, we have practiced and practiced and practiced to get to where we are today. Regardless of whether or not we're happy with the result. Who's been living our life if it hasn't been us? We are the masters and experts in our lives: in the successes, the failures, what works, and what doesn't. Our lives, as we are accustomed to living them, are our comfort zones; they are our routines or our habits. Our successes and failures may be as a result of living unconsciously and we may feel that we're on a ride called life and not actually feel like we have any control or say with what happens to us.

So if the way we are living our lives currently is our routine; then our current way of existing is our comfort zone. We are experts in this field, no matter what it entails: whether healthy, productive, destructive, etc. Introducing something new to our routine can be likened to 'going off script' in the movie analogy, however, most of us are not good at 'going off script' and we will always find our way back to our previous routines. Therefore, we need to build new routines and devise a new script in order to change the way we live and lead our lives.

To Summarize

Language shapes our present and future. The way we use it, think about it, speak it, and what we believe about it is all of great importance.

Remember, we're not striving toward perfection but we are striving toward progression. We are here to ***Strive To Optimize*** as many processes within our lives as possible so that we can be all that we believe we can be and so that we achieve all that we believe we can achieve.

One of the best ideas I've heard about approaching change is through addition. So much of the time we focus on the absence of something instead of the presence of something else. Focusing on the absence of something actually puts our attention onto the thing that we supposedly don't want and it becomes more difficult to do anything other than that thing we don't want. Here's an example. Let's say you eat ice cream everyday and you want to stop. If you focus on avoiding ice cream it becomes a fight to try and avoid it. Instead of focusing on *not* eating ice cream turn your focus onto something you could *add* to your life that would positively impact it. Maybe you want to start exercising or eating healthier. So instead focus on going for a walk or eating a bunch of raw carrots before you would typically sit down to eat your ice cream. If you practice adding things to your life and stay committed you'll notice that you end up crowding out the things you wanted to stop in the first place.

One of the greatest benefits of the Four C Process is that it's so intuitive. We've all done it and we've all *already* been successful using this process. It's the foundation of all great success in your life, whether you know it or not.

This approach will work if you're developing a business relationship with a potential client, why? Because *you have to show you're interested in them*. If you're a teacher, a supervisor, a CEO, a manager, an entrepreneur, a parent, a child, a coach, absolutely anyone and everyone. The Four C Process is the exact way you would develop a relationship with *ANYONE!* If you're interested in going out with someone what do you have to do? You have to be curious about the other person. So you ask them out and then learn a whole bunch about them. If both of you want to continue you cultivate the relationship and go out again and you're still curious so you're still discovering more about the other person and you continue to cultivate and 'back and forth' you go learning about one another and slowly but surely building up beneath the scenes is confidence. You become confident in knowing the other person, their character, their values, their interests, etc. and if your relationship continues to mature you'll collaborate together by going on trips together, as an example. The most obvious form of collaboration in a relationship would be getting married and/or wanting to collaborate on living your life together.

In a business relationship, this would work very similarly. The client is interested in your business or you are interested in taking the client on, or both. You are curious about the client and the client is curious about you. You ask each other questions, learn about each other and each other's businesses (you cultivate the relationship). If confidence develops and you have confidence in the client and the client has confidence in you, guess what? You collaborate with one another and the client decides to purchase your services.

The applications of the Four C Process are absolutely endless. It is absolutely essential to the success of any friendship, personal relationship, partnership, business relationship, teacher-student relationship, parent-child relationship, coach-athlete relationship, artist-student relationship, and so on, and so on, and so on.

It's Time To Get Into The Driver's Seat

For too long we've been the passengers in the vehicle of our lives, somewhat guiding our lives, whether consciously or unconsciously along the roads of our lives. Or even worse, some of us are in the rear-facing children's car seats looking out the back window of where we've been but with no idea where we're going. Even worse still for these individuals is they feel as if they have no control over the direction their life is taking. They're just along for the ride.

It's time to get back in the driver's seat, grip the steering wheel firmly, and confidently steer our lives in the direction that we want to go. We're tired of being passengers. We have to be wary of our unconscious mind who always likes to drive. It's got loads of feedback loops that prevent our conscious minds from getting back in the driver's seat. Become conscious of any dependencies that subtract from our physical, mental, emotional, or spiritual well being because they'll definitely be in the driver's seat. In these instances we feel helpless to change anything in our lives.

Do you want to drive? Do you want to steer your life in the direction you want to go so you can be in a place where you want to be? Well, I've got to tell you where we have to start but you're not going to like it. The problem is that we're so used to getting things immediately, to instant gratification; we want immediate responses to our text messages, we want immediate likes and comments on our social media posts, we want one-day shipping on all orders. We want things to be made, done, and completed as quickly and easily as possible while putting in as little effort as we possibly can. Let me be clear, there is nothing that somebody is going to give you or even can give you that is immediately going to teleport you to the place you want to be.

Guess what, you have to start here. Right now in this moment and you've got to be ready to do more than just wish. If you're not taking action you're just fantasizing about a reality that will never be because you're not doing anything to get there.

So who's ready to take action? Who's ready to get into the driver's seat of *the car* of *your own life* and take it to places you've always wanted to.

Alright then, *LET'S GO!*

The Finish… Or Is It The Beginning?

Ahhhh, what better way to finish than with a question. In the end the choice is always left up to *you*. What do you want from life? Because whether you know it or not you're already getting what you've been asking for and if it's something that *you* don't want in *your life* then the only person you need to talk to is staring back at you in the mirror. Are you happy with what you see? If so fantastic! If not, then you've got to shed some light on that unconscious mind of yours because it's getting in the way of your brilliance! Yeah, that's right! Your Brilliance! You are brilliant! Just the way you are. You're just being overshadowed by your unconscious mind. That's okay. There's time.

Reignite the fire of curiosity that is still at work somewhere inside of you and don't stop listening to that fire. Use your conscious mind to keep adding oxygen and fuel to the fire and burn, baby, burn! *Light it up!*

I'll finish with a poem/rap I wrote last year, and if you're not pumped up enough about getting curious, cultivating, becoming *more* confident (or just recognizing the ways that you already *are*), and collaborating with others then this will definitely get you there!

Don't let anything stop you from allowing your light to shine as bright as it wants to and is capable of!

Visualize

Those Thoughts of which you theorize

What you want to materialize

From sunrise to sunrise

Forget about the hows, whats, whos, or whys

Only time is now because time flies

Stop telling yourself the same old lies

Time to stop with the cries

And stop with the sighs

Get your life in order, organize

Take your junk and minimize

Take your passion and maximize

Don't let doubts continue to jeopardize

Don't let thoughts continue to paralyze

Don't accept the status quo and rationalize

Life is here for us to create and personalize

So get your goals and categorize

Stop sitting there, don't apologize

Time to shape up and recognize

The time is now to get wise

Grasp those dreams, act now, and improvise

Never look back and always shoot for the skies

Peace

About The Author

Mike has undergraduate degrees in Life Sciences and Social Work, as well as a graduate degree in Social Work. He's had different jobs over the years and has been writing on the side, never really fully believing or committing to his real passions and strengths for empowering others. He developed the ideas in this book over the course of the last fourteen months. He finally followed his own advice in the Four C Process and completed this book. He started his business, Stick To Your Core Consulting, in order to help others achieve everything they've always wanted to simply by sticking to the core of who they are: their strengths, their abilities, their skills, their values, and their own inner wisdom.

When he's not writing, speaking, and working one on one with others you'll find him in the pool, on the bike, or on the trails training for marathons, ultramarathons, triathlons, and ironmans; pushing his mind, body, and spirit to see how far it can take him. He believes there really are no limits, only the ones we set for ourselves.

CPSIA information can be obtained
at www.ICGtesting.com
Printed in the USA
FFOW03n2147270318
46074870-47057FF